# The Jeweler's Guide to
# EFFECTIVE
# INSURANCE APPRAISING

# The Jeweler's Guide to EFFECTIVE INSURANCE APPRAISING

RALPH S. JOSEPH

Gemworld International, Inc.
Northbrook, Illinois

*This book is dedicated to my parents, Abe and Lillian Joseph.*

*Thanks for your love and generosity, and the faith you demonstrated even when I doubted myself.*

*You got me started in business and helped me through the hard times.*

*I am grateful that you can share the joy of this accomplishment.*

As the chief training consultant for more than 150 retail jewelry firms with nearly one billion dollars in retail sales, and as a former director of the Gemological Institute of America, I have had the opportunity to conduct research and training in more than one hundred cities around the world, working directly with many thousands of individuals in our industry. I am constantly bewildered by the number of these people who dramatically under utilize their talents and resources. These are educated people who know what they should be doing, and why they should be doing it, yet continually fail to follow through. As stated in the author's introduction, we in the industry know we should be more professional with our insurance appraisals. We know the potentially dangerous consequences when we are not, yet we make the same mistakes again and again.

So how do we change our behavior and achieve the success that we would like to have? It is possible to double our incomes and current levels of success if we can commit to the following two fundamental principles: clarity of purpose and self-discipline.

To have clarity of purpose, we must first project our thoughts into the future in an attempt to determine our desired outcome. Since we are projecting into the future, anything is possible. If you could create your own success, what would it be? What would it look like? How would it feel? How would you act? Who would you need to be in the coming months and years to bring about the reality of your imaginings? The answers to these and other similar questions can give you some powerful references to use in order to create the clarity of purpose you need for success.

Clarity of purpose is one way of referring to what is also called "having vision," and is often seen as a concept reserved for CEOs and other top-level executives. But we all need the benefit of this kind of vision. We all need to know where we are going. Imagine trying to drive to work with the equivalent of a thick coat of black paint covering your windshield. When your destination isn't clear, how can you possibly know where you are heading? How can you achieve success if you don't know what your goals are or how you are going to reach them?

The other major obstacle that often prevents talented people from realizing their potential is lack of self-discipline. Part of the problem is cultural. We currently live in a society where we avoid acceptance of responsibility for our actions, and instead see ourselves as victims of circumstance. We think that we can make poor choices and then blame third parties—our parents, our teachers, our employers—for the outcomes of our decisions. But the truth is, if you are going to control your own destiny, you have to accept responsibility for your decisions and subsequent actions. When you accept responsibility for your behavior, and make choices because you know they are right, not because they are easy, you are exercising self-discipline. And when you do that consistently, you are in control of your future.

So there you have it. Without clarity of purpose, the majority of us wander around without defined goals, wondering why we are not experiencing desired levels of success. We know what is right to do, and what we need to do, but without self-discipline, we fail to follow through. And then we wonder why others are so lucky and get all the breaks.

Ralph Joseph has written a book to remind all of us in the jewelry industry what are the right things to do in the insurance appraisal business. Most of us are already familiar with the basic concepts and needs. Yet so many of us in the industry, rather than behave professionally, still choose to cut corners and skip the details for the sake of convenience. However, if your customer experiences a loss, and your appraisal interferes with the insurance company's ability to properly settle the claim, that customer is hurt. It is your future and your ultimate success or failure. Just how professional do you envision yourself to be? If you take the time to read this book and apply its principles, you will discover a set of guidelines to use in building your professionalism and your business success.

Kevin G. Moody, G.G.
Training Strategist and Consultant

Uniform Standards of Professional Appraisal Practice (USPAP) were developed in 1986/87 by a group called The Appraisal Foundation from a need of the Federal government during the Savings & Loan crisis to establish and promulgate nationwide standards which would benefit both appraisers and users of appraisal services. Since that time these standards have become the common denominator that connects almost all the appraisal organizations in the United States-including those in the personal property fields such as jewelry. Most banking institutions, all Federal agencies, and many insurance carriers now insist upon appraisals that conform to USPAP. Indeed, the trend continues to gain momentum and may someday include all appraisals done for any purpose or use.

Although primarily established as a reaction to real estate problems, two standards of the ten deal specifically with the development of a personal property appraisal (Section 7) and the reporting of those results (Section 8). These requirements and guidelines cover much of what is taught by the major appraisal organizations in their methodology and principle courses, but leave the employment of the correct techniques to the trained and qualified appraiser. A qualified appraiser is not one that does appraisals, but one who has been trained properly to do appraisals "right". One is not "grandfathered" into the appraisal profession by virtue of a lifetime of repeated bad experience. The qualified appraiser not only passes strict criteria in both the appraisal methodology and subject matter, but continuously improves their skills on a daily basis to remain proficient. Appraisers are not adjunct self taught dealers or store owners, but professionals with their own field of endeavor. Those not willing to submit to rigorous training and testing should leave the skill to others who will.

The Appraisal Foundation, headquartered in Washington, is not a Federal Appraisal Membership organization. It oversees the Appraisal Standards Board that alters, amends, and interprets the Uniform Standard for the industry and the public. State and federal regulatory authorities may enforce the standards through their individual spheres of influence. Appraisal organizations have input to the Appraisal Standards Board that meets on a regular basis. One does not belong to "USPAP," but provides appraisal services that meet USPAP regulations.

USPAP information is covered by most appraisal organizations and courses are held around the country that include both the combined real estate/personal property sections and some that deal strictly with personal property. Licensing of personal property appraisers by USPAP testing does not yet exist. Many USPAP courses, however, provide "certificates of completions" or Continuing Education Units (CEU). Check with your individual associations. These credentials should be noted on all curriculum vitaes or resumes which are included in any appraisal.

The need for USPAP in the jewelry profession is certainly apparent. Most of what passes today for a jewelry appraisal falls far short of these standards, even in a very limited sense. Store receipts, pre-printed "certificates of appraisal," and prices written on a store's letterhead do not constitute even the shadow of a reliable appraisal and in fact, promote misleading and misunderstood reports—the type that caused USPAP to be developed in the first place.

What are the correct elements of a USPAP appraisal? A careful read of Mr. Joseph's book will lead you in the right direction. They include statements about purpose and intended use, the cornerstones of every appraisal endeavor. Reports should include a detailed list of the limiting conditions under which the task was performed, as well as explanations covering the collection, verification, and reconciliation of all the data. Need we say the description must be adequate, clear, and definitive? Is there a stated method of identification and the correct valuation approach? Are markets appropriate for the use? Have they been identified and defined to be understood by the client? Has the effect of highest and best use been measured by analyzing the current and alternative uses? Is all this and more part of your normal appraisal routine?

How many write a very brief description of the jewelry with a one line code and follow with a ball park guess of selling price? Do we really consider effects on value caused by attributes such as condition, style, quality, manufacturer, artist, materials, origin, age, provenance, etc.? Yet USPAP states all such pertinent information is part of the development of a normal (jewelry) appraisal.

USPAP speaks to the format of the actual report as well. In fact, USPAP appraisals must contain a certification which includes a statement of truth and fact, prospective interest (if any), a contingent compensations clause, personal inspection and responsibility claims, and a USPAP confirmation statement. How many current jewelry appraisals even hint to any of the above?

The fact that many jewelry appraisals are done by those who sell the piece to the client indicates a present interest in the property. The "appraisals" that are done carry no certification stating the personal bias of the appraiser. This is not permitted. In addition, "oral" appraisals must include all the substantive matters that apply to written appraisals. Such adoption by the jewelry profession would certainly eliminate a large portion of all appraisals. Those done would be done correctly.

"If a thing is worth doing, it should be worth doing right." For those who desire to offer jewelry appraisals as part of their service, a commitment must be made for education, training, and renewal. It may seem like an oppressive mountain of red tape, but only to those who would rather rely upon guesswork, meaningless jargon, and unsubstantiated values.

Appraisal standards are not options, like membership in the choice of a specific appraisal organization, nor are they delicacies for the rich and famous. They are necessities bound by consumers who trust our profession to provide educated, impartial, and qualified valuations that protect their possessions and by appraisers who seek the common good of holding forth a level playing field where the rules are the same for all players

Copies of USPAP '96 are available by writing The Appraisal Foundation, 1029 Vermont Avenue NW Suite 900, Washington, DC 20005-3517.


Leon Castner, CAPP, Ph.D., AAA
Senior Partner National Appraisal Consultants
Hope, New Jersey

When I was first approached to write this book, I responded with a host of self-directed questions. The most important was, "Who would the book be for?" Of course I wanted to have a book published, but why? As previous authors of appraisal books would no doubt agree, such books are not big money makers—so that couldn't be the allure.

In my twenty-plus years in our unique industry, my experience has been broad and varied. I worked for relatives in a mom-and-pop store for twelve years. I became one of two "pops" myself for six years, having purchased the business with a partner. During that tenure of ownership, issues of value became important to me personally and, more importantly, to the business and its loyal customers.

I entered into appraising by accident. As owners, my partner and I were not comfortable turning down *any* business—let alone appraisals. We knew that the handwritten so-called appraisals scribbled on a form developed by a business forms company were not adequate. We also knew that we didn't have a clue when it came to appraising. So, we made the choice most jewelers make—we did appraisals anyway.

As is the case with most appraisers who have now attained some degree of enlightenment, I shudder when I think about those early documents. I had legitimate doubts about them even back then, when I didn't really understand the appraisal process. Did my appraisals really protect my clients? Was the item identified sufficiently to allow an insurance company to settle a claim? Should photographs be included? Did I have to be a gemologist to write appraisals properly? Is the stated value the most important ingredient? What will other jewelers say about these appraisals when they see them?

I reached a point where I could no longer ignore the appraisal issues—I was too insecure about what I was doing. I knew almost nothing about insurance. I knew next to nothing about gemology. And I knew *absolutely* nothing of what was then the infant appraisal profession. But that was 1985. Looking back, I suppose at the time very few jewelers knew any better than I did.

Now, years later, many jewelers do know better. Although relatively few have taken advantage of the educational opportunities available through organizations such as the International Society of Appraisers (ISA), the American Society of Appraisers (ASA), the American Gem Society (AGS), and the National Association of Jewelry Appraisers (NAJA), there is awareness that such programs exist.

I decided to restrict this work to insurance for several reasons. For one, insurance is an exceptional rather than a typical kind of appraising, because the appraisal itself serves as the basis for a contract. This contract between the insured and the insurance company sets the stage for indemnifying or restoring the policy holder in the event of a loss.

That insurance appraising is the exception to most appraisal methodology rather than the rule is news to most jewelers. We often hear retailers talk about the fact that they only do "simple insurance appraisals," so they don't need any "fancy education." Jewelers generally feel safe if they restrict themselves to insurance appraising and replacement value. This false sense of security is partly derived from the belief many jewelers have that, "I know the market. I deal in these things every day." In the most minor way that belief is valid. But there's so much more. In fact, methodology for fair market value appraising such as that done for estates is much more straightforward, which contradicts the general opinion on the subject. If fair market value is employed properly, it is defined for the appraiser (with variations according to legal jurisdiction), and the valuation job is fairly straightforward. If a definition of fair market value tells us to research an item in its "most common market," for sales between "willing buyers and willing sellers, neither being compelled to act, and both being reasonably knowledgeable of the relevant facts," and further tells us that these sales must be "to the ultimate consumer," and that prices paid by dealers "for resale of the item in its present form" are unacceptable comparables, our parameters are narrowed for us.*

But insurance valuation is, in a sense (and I use this term advisedly) negotiable. Because theoretically, policy holders and insurance companies can contract for anything. A college basketball star can insure his ankles against an injury which would jeopardize projected future earnings. There's no telling what such a policy would cost, but certainly if the two parties can agree on a coverage amount, covered perils, and a premium amount, the policy can be written. And so it is in theory with jewelry.

Therefore, the fate of both parties is in the appraiser's hands. Insurance underwriters cannot be expected to read every appraisal word for word, then determine if values are accurate. They can only look for signals that indicate problem issues. And because they are not jewelers, only the most blatant warning signs are obvious to them.

As an insurance replacement specialist, I see the damage done by inadequate appraisals. Missing details in item descriptions, overstated values used at the time of purchase to show customers what a "bargain" they received, omitted photographs, and illegible hand-scribbled words, can all cause problems when a loss occurs.

Because most jewelry insurance policies allow the insurer to shop for replacement items at the time of the loss, your descriptive information is critical. It is not only the basis for determining the nature of the loss, it is the adjuster's bible regarding that item. It is all the insurance company has to work with. That is why an entire chapter of this book is devoted to item descriptions and the descriptive elements that I think are critical to effective insurance appraisals.

This book is not intended to be a substitute for appraisal education. The interaction encountered in classroom appraisal courses, and to a lesser but still significant degree the comprehensive picture presented in quality home study courses, are highly recommended as the proper way to learn appraising.

This book is offered as a means of opening the door to professional insurance appraising for jewelers, while encouraging readers to seek more knowledge. A highly respected fellow appraiser once said to me that someone should write an appraisal book for the jeweler who

*This brief overview of fair market value is not all inclusive, and the subject is not dealt with in this book. It is simply noted here to help make and clarify a point. As an aside, it also should remind readers that extensive education and understanding of the principles involved are necessary before taking on fmv assignments.

decorates his own display windows...and washes them too. I hope this book proves valuable to that jeweler, and also to those with larger or smaller businesses.

*The Jeweler's Guide to Effective Insurance Appraising* is a manual—a handbook intended to guide the reader through the process of writing credible insurance appraisals. There is no complete substitute for a sound and thorough education, and the experience to complement it.

My hope is that my work will help you to elevate the level at which you perform this important service. If it accomplishes that, it elevates all of us professionally, and makes our entire industry look better in the eyes of the public. I hope my experiences, from take-in to delivery, will help you to better serve the customers you value so highly.

RSJ

*With thanks*

**This book would not be complete without thanking the many professionals whose assistance, encouragement, and support I appreciate so much.**

Jim Coote, selective technical editor
Richard Drucker, publisher, conceptual editor
William Hoefer, Jr., technical editor
John Jaeger, technical editor
Faye Joseph, text editor
Robert Shaw, selective technical editor

Cos Altobelli
Doris Cardinal
Leon Castner
Lynn Diamond
Ray Di Giovanni
Maurice Fry
The Gemological Institute of America
Steve Getzoff
Al Gilbertson
Charles and the late Ruth Goldman
Robert Goldman
Scott Gordon
Lael Hagen
Dianne Harman
George Holmes
The International Society of Appraisers (ISA)
Sue Johnson
Ken Joseph
Brian Kathenes
Don Kay
Gail Levine
Elaine Luartes
Fred Michmershuizen
Kevin Moody
*National Jeweler*

Danusia Niklewicz
New Jersey Jewelers Association
Patsy, Jan and Terri, from the old ISA office
Jon Phillips
Jonathan Price
Christie Romero
Elly Rosen
Dr. and Mrs. Steve Ross
David Rotenberg
Howard Rubin
The Scull Group
Abe Sherman
Greg Sherman
The Staff at Abe Sherman Fine Jewelry
Pearl Shiffman
Whitney Sielaff
Sherry Skillman
Leonard Smith, Esq.
Lisa Snelgrove
Pierre Tardy
Harold Tivol
Treasure Group International
Starla Turner
Thom and Lynn Underwood
William Whetstone

And of course, thank you to the many friends, family, and colleagues whose names could have filled another page or two.

# Table of Contents

Chapter 1      *You Can Make a Difference*
               **The Positive Philosophy of Appraising** . . . . . . . . . . . . . . . . . . . . .*1*

Chapter 2      *This Chapter does not Belong in this Book*
               **Statement of Sale and Evaluation for Insurance** . . . . . . . . . .*11*

Chapter 3      *The Big Bad Wolf, or Little Red Riding Hood?*
               **A Few Words About Insurance Companies** . . . . . . . . . . . . . . .*19*

Chapter 4      *Up Periscope*
               **The Role of Gemology in Appraising** . . . . . . . . . . . . . . . . . .*25*

Chapter 5      *So What is it Worth?*
               **Arriving at a Reasonable Estimate of Value** . . . . . . . . . . . .*33*

Chapter 6      *Retail is Retail, so What is the Big Deal?*
               **Retail Markets and their Implications** . . . . . . . . . . . . . . . . .*41*

Chapter 7      *Nuts and Bolts*
               **Anatomy of the Insurance Appraisal, Part I** . . . . . . . . . . . .*47*

Chapter 8      *Soup to Nuts*
               **Anatomy of the Insurance Appraisal, Part II** . . . . . . . . . . . .*59*

Chapter 9      *Hyping the Typing*
               **Generating the Document** . . . . . . . . . . . . . . . . . . . . . . . . .*73*

Chapter 10     *A Matter of Form*
               **Pre-printed Forms and How They Can Help** . . . . . . . . . . .*79*

Chapter 11     *The Stated Value is Accurate, so What else Matters?*
               **The Basics of Insurance Replacement** . . . . . . . . . . . . . . . .*95*

Chapter 12     *Bottom Line, Does it Add to My Bottom Line?*
               **Organizing and Selling your Appraisal Services** . . . . . . . . .*109*

Chapter 13     *Uh-Oh, This One is Different!*
               **Unusual Scenarios and How to Handle Them** . . . . . . . . . .*119*

Chapter 14     *Nobody Cares About Appraising*
               **Generating Support for Professional Appraisal Practices** . . . . . .*127*

Chapter 15     *The Truth is Out There Somewhere...*
               **A Few Words About Non-Insurance Appraising** . . . . . . . . .*131*

Chapter 16     *All that is Left, is to do What is Right*
               **Ethical Considerations for Insurance Appraisals** . . . . . . . .*137*

Chapter 17     *To Every Appraisal, Learn, Learn, Learn, There is a Reason, Learn, Learn, Learn*
               **Education–The Great De-Equalizer** . . . . . . . . . . . . . . . . . .*145*

Post Script    Some Final Thoughts About Appraising . . . . . . . . . . . . . . . . . . . .*151*

Addendum:      Organizations . . . . . . . . . . . . . . . . . . . . . . . . . . . . . . . . . . . .*153*

Addendum:      Sample Appraisal . . . . . . . . . . . . . . . . . . . . . . . . . . . . . . . . . .*155*

Index          . . . . . . . . . . . . . . . . . . . . . . . . . . . . . . . . . . . . . . . . . . . . .*171*

# *1* *You Can Make a Difference....*

# The Positive Philosophy of Appraising

C an you truly say that most of your clients over the past several years would seek you out first if they required appraisal services? How much positive feedback do you receive? Does an examination of your appraisal by the client make it abundantly clear that you have served that client uniquely well?

Many of the appraisal clients you work with will tell you about negative experiences with insurance claims. In virtually all cases, the stories you hear will hinge upon the quality—or lack of quality—of the appraisal used to assess the loss and process the insurance claim.

A client in Los Angeles several years ago, upon seeing a sample of my work, asked a common question: "Do I really need all of that detail?" She wondered if item descriptions could be less detailed and if photographs could be eliminated in order to decrease the fee. My response was straightforward. "If you know for a fact that you will never sustain a loss of any of your jewelry, then I would say you do not require this much detail. In fact, you need neither the appraisal nor the insurance. But unless you know this absolutely, I assume you are buying the insurance because of the possibility of a future loss— in which case you will need as much detail as possible to help you and your claims adjuster determine proper compensation as per your insurance policy." She agreed to the appraisal, performed completely and properly, and to the appropriate fee.

Nearly a year later I heard from this client again. Her home had been burgled while she was out of the country. Her insurance claims adjuster told her that it had been "the easiest jewelry claim" he had ever handled, specifically because of the way in which the appraisal had been performed.

A great deal can be learned from this experience. First, do not sacrifice the quality of your appraisal and doing the job correctly for the sake of saving a client money. Second, remember that appraising is truly a service to the public. In the past, and to some degree even now, jewelers felt guilty about charging for appraisals, and frequently provided free appraising in much the same way as they provided free gift-wrapping. My client's experience taught me not only that I did not have to feel guilty about charging a fee, but also that the proper job was worth what might be considered, to the uninitiated, a large fee. From a confidence standpoint, that woman's loss was my everlasting gain as an appraiser.

### *You are confident in your work, and convinced that appraising is a valuable professional service. So how much should you charge?*

The question about fees is frequently asked during classes and seminars on appraising. One of the salient points of this entire book is that we must become professional appraisers—or not appraise at all. Being a professional appraiser means that we charge a professional fee. This book will not tell you specifically *what* to charge, but rather, *how* you charge, and how you decide upon a fee structure.

This discussion is not meant to establish standard pricing, or even to suggest how much you might charge. Yet some kind of reference point will be helpful in discussing fees. So please understand that the dollar amounts are not specific to any particular appraiser's practice, nor are they suggested fees—they are simply examples.

Your fee structure should be consistent. You do not want to charge $35.00 to appraise an item today, then charge $85.00 for a similar item two weeks later. Such fee changes can only raise suspicion, as your clients become aware of inconsistencies—even if they are unintentional. Your fees should be based upon something you can reasonably track and repeat.

Some appraisers charge an hourly fee. This is fairly straightforward. For example, they may charge $40.00 per hour for their own time, and possibly less for secretarial or clerical time (even if they act as their own secretary). Time expenditures are tracked, and a bill is prepared accordingly. In order to do this fairly, however, most appraisers, particularly those in the retail jewelry business, would have to use a stopwatch, clicking it off and on for every interruption and resumption of work. This creates an unacceptable burden for many appraisers, particularly if they do not have clerical support. To combat this problem, consider billing in minimum fifteen minute segments. This eliminates the need to track things like minute-long telephone calls.

---

## SAMPLE INVOICE

### INVOICE FOR APPRAISAL SERVICES RENDERED
### R. Joseph Appraisal Co.
91263 Diamond Blvd., Suite 5153
Hometown, NJ 08888
(609) 123-4567

**Dr. and Mrs. Ross Stevens**
**918 Princeton Avenue**
**Harvard, New Jersey 08887**

| | | |
|---|---|---|
| Consultation: | 1.5 hours @ $50/hour | $75.00 |
| Research and and documentation: | 3.75 hours @ $50/hour | 187.50 |
| Secretarial: | 1.25 hours @ $20/hour | 25.00 |
| Long distance telephone and fax: | | 11.25 |
| **TOTAL AMOUNT DUE:** | | **$298.75** |

*Thank you for allowing us to serve you.*

---

Hourly billing seems to work best for someone who can work in uninterrupted blocks of time. Of course, appraising requires concentration and is best handled in this manner anyway. Hourly billing, however, may limit your ability to quote an exact fee in advance. Many clients will prefer to know just how much they will be charged before you begin work. If you do choose to bill hourly, be sure to log your time and all your expenses carefully, and make that record part of the file for each client and assignment.

There *are* assignments that can easily be quoted strictly by the hour. You may receive calls from attorneys, bank officers, and other professionals who require your services. These kinds of assignments often require large blocks of (trackable) time, such as for specific research, documentation, testimony, or consulting. This time is easy to track, and professionals usually need to know how much they're spending while the clock is running. So in these cases it may be easy and practical to quote an hourly rate, and to keep track of time in a detailed log. You may even choose to quote a minimum fee for a brief consultation that you expect to take just a few minutes, or perhaps an hour or two. Consider quoting a minimum fee, or requiring a non-refundable retainer.

Some appraisers prefer to charge by the item. They may charge, for example, $30.00 for the first item, and $10.00 for each item thereafter. The rationale is that there is a certain amount of time and energy involved in doing any appraisal, so the fee for the first item has to be sufficient to cover that time and effort. This is a viable option, and no doubt the most consistent and easy for a client to understand and trust, but there are difficulties with this method of fee structuring. For example, several complicated items included in one appraisal would result in a loss to the appraiser. Yet if an appraisal involves only very simple items, such as plain gold chains and bracelets, it may appear to a client that there has been an overcharge. If this method of fee structuring appeals to you, set the charges you decide upon as minimums only, with adjustments to be made for particularly difficult or easy items.

You might want to consider combining the two types of fee structures. You could, for example, charge by the job, quoting for the entire project after seeing the jewelry. This method relies on experience with many types of jewelry. With experience, you will be able to look at one item or many items, and quote the fee quickly and accurately based upon several factors. How much gemological examination and documentation is required? Does an item contain fifty diamonds with four or five different cutting styles, variable sizes, and a wide range of quality? Or is this a half carat diamond solitaire in a plain gold mounting?

Additionally, some items carry increased responsibility and liability because of their greater value. Just as GIA's Gem Trade Laboratory charges higher fees for larger diamonds, many appraisers develop a sliding scale for diamond appraisals. For example, $40.00 up to 0.50 carat, $60.00 up to one carat, $90.00 up to 1.50 carats, and so on up to a particular size, beyond which you can quote each appraisal job according to the particular circumstances involved. Remember, increasing value means increasing responsibility—and liability. Charging a higher fee when your responsibility is greater is ethical and makes sense. This is not the same as charging a percentage of value, which is detailed later in this chapter. Charging a percentage displays an obvious and undeniable conflict of interest, and amounts to a contingency fee. Most people would at least be tempted to overstate value if the result was an automatic fee increase. Even the *perception* that this is the case can be damaging to your reputation.

When setting fees, ask yourself, "Will there be any extensive research required?" Obviously a greater charge will be required for an antique bracelet by Louis-Francois Cartier than for a contemporary bracelet of a generic nature. Certainly appraisers who are actively involved in the marketplace do not have to go out to find a comparable sale to justify their value conclusion for every item being appraised. However, what about that bracelet by Louis-Francois Cartier?

Gemologically there may be very little required of your time. But research may involve hours and hours, perhaps over several weeks or months. This research must be taken into account if you are to be properly compensated for your time and expertise. Rather than be tempted to do a less than professional job because you "cannot possibly charge enough to do so" (a phrase commonly voiced by appraisal students), why not do a wonderful job and charge a commensurate fee? Professional appraisers would rather give up a job than knowingly perform poorly.

The fees you charge should reflect your opinion of the value of your time, so that you are comfortable quoting and justifying those fees. No doubt you quote and charge repair fees and have developed a merchandise pricing system that you are comfortable with. If you think these fees are too high or too low, it would seem natural to reassess your pricing structure. Appraising should be no different. Charge what you think your time—your appraisal

## Deposition Supposition

Some appraisers quote a minimum charge for deposition; for example, two hours at their current hourly rate. On occasion this fee arrangement is challenged by opposing counsel. One particular challenge was directed at an appraiser immediately prior to deposition. Opposing counsel presented him with a check for the second half of his minimum fee for appearing, having protested the quote by sending only half originally. "I am giving you this without editorial comment," he noted dryly. "None required," was the appraiser's simple response, "and I accept it without an editorial reply." This set the tone for a loving relationship between the two, as you might imagine. The whole scenario might have been avoided had the appraiser simply quoted a flat fee "portal to portal," plus an hourly fee rate for time actually spent in deposition.

At the beginning of the deposition itself, the appraiser was asked, "Do you charge a minimum fee for a deposi tion?" He responded that he did. "And what is that minimum fee?" was the next question. The appraiser said that he charged a two hour minimum at X dollars per hour, because by the time he left his office, drove to even a local site for a deposition, parked, and drove back, nearly an hour was spent just in transportation time (if you have driven in any major city, you know how true this is). The transportation time was exclusive of the time he was testifying under oath. His explanation concluded with, "It is just not worth leaving my office and losing other potential business if I am not guaranteed a minimum amount. I quoted this fee in advance, and you asked to take my deposition, so I do not quite know why you are asking these questions now." The deposition proceeded, and the appraiser walked away with his fee, paid in full. Again, this was laid out in advance, and any additional time could have been easily documented and billed accordingly. In any event, always understand your fee structure thoroughly—because it will almost always be discussed if you have to testify under oath.

"merchandise"— is worth, and be comfortable with it. Logistically, it is preferable to do fewer appraisals for more money, rather than working harder for the same or less income.

When quoting fees, you might also want to lay out the terms for payment. You might require full payment in advance, partial payment in advance and the balance due upon delivery of the appraisal, or a partial payment with an agreement to bill for the balance. There are some obvious advantages to each method, and choosing is a personal matter. One less obvious advantage to billing for the balance: If you bill payable 30 days after the appraisal is completed, you might be able to successfully argue that your Appraisal Information Document (AID, sometimes known as a cover letter, please see Chapters 7 and 8) is contractual, because your client had sufficient time in which to read it before submitting payment. On the other hand, being paid in advance saves the time and expense associated with billing.

One additional note about setting fees. It is unethical to charge a percentage of stated value as your fee. The reason is obvious. If you are charging, for example, 2% of value as a fee, and have the option to state a value of $10,000.00 or $12,000.00 on a particular item, there is a $40.00 advantage to you to go with the higher number. As stated earlier, even the most honest person might be tempted to overstate value to increase the fee. And even if you are above that temptation, rest assured that the perception will be otherwise. This practice can only raise suspicion, and courts have rejected testimony when such bias is evident. Increased liability, however, does justify a higher fee. As noted earlier, it is acceptable ethically to set a sliding scale, for example, according to diamond size. As long as the fee is not tied to value specifically, a conflict of interest does not exist. A ten carat diamond (regardless of quality or value) would warrant a higher fee than a 1/4 carat diamond, because of the higher degree of care required, and the increased liability that comes with the larger diamond.

### *Quoting Fees to the Public*

If you choose the combined fee structure I described earlier—a by-the-job fee based upon a per-item foundation—quoting fees is a bit more involved than if you charge a straight hourly or per-item fee. This fee structure will require some training of your staff if you have employees, and even some self-training if you work alone. When asked about fees, employees who are not involved in the appraisal process should explain that "fees are set by the appraiser, who will call you [the client] prior to beginning work on your jewelry."

Consider this sample statement as a response to a query about your fees, when the jewelry is not available for inspection (a telephone inquiry, for example): "We charge a *minimum* of $35.00 for the first item, and a *minimum* of $20.00 for each additional item." Emphasize the word **minimum**, otherwise nine out of ten clients will automatically come in prepared to pay $20.00 for any one item. Continue, saying: "Many items exceed the minimum charge, so please understand that you will be charged at least what you are quoted on the phone, and perhaps more. Fees are based upon the complexity of the items themselves, and the amount of research and clerical time involved in the preparation of the appraisal. All of these elements are related to the nature of the appraisal as well. For example, insurance, estate tax, and appraisal for resale may have different ramifications regarding the appraiser's time and effort. In some cases, at our discretion, we may even charge a bit less than the minimum...for example, if you have several plain gold chains, we would not charge the stated minimum for each."

It is also a good idea to emphasize that there will be no surprises regarding charges for appraisal services. All fees should be quoted exactly, or estimated including a *maximum charge*, in advance. It is recommended that you agree upon the fee in writing (please see Chapter 10), so there is no question later.

I once received a call from a frantic appraiser, Mr. Careless, who had just finished an appraisal for an old high school friend he had been reunited with at a dinner party. Their conversation had led to Ms. Oldfriend's need to have 75 pieces of jewelry appraised. Mr. Careless assured her that he would "take it easy" with regard to the fee, and the two arranged to get together. Ms. Oldfriend dropped off the jewelry, and a week later Mr. Careless called to say the jewelry and the finished appraisal could be retrieved.

When Ms. Oldfriend arrived, she was presented with a bill for $1200.00. She was flabbergasted, and declared, "I had no idea it would be this expensive!!" Mr. Careless assured her that he would normally charge $1800.00, and that he had indeed kept his promise of a substantial discount. Ms. Oldfriend quickly became the appraiser's enemy, and insisted upon taking her jewelry—but refused to pay for the appraisal. Stunned and caught off guard, Mr. Careless watched her leave with her jewelry, and, in a sense, his $1200.00.

After listening to this story and learning that no specific fee had been quoted in advance, not even verbally, let alone in writing, I told Mr. Careless that he needed the advice of an attorney, and not that of a fellow appraiser. I never followed up on the resolution of this dispute, but it seems reasonable to assume that it was unsatisfactory to at least one of the parties.

So, what does all of this talk about fees have to do with a positive philosophy of appraising? Consumers of appraisals are ultimately sensitive to two main elements. One, will the appraisal meet their needs? Tied into this of course, is the issue of properly informing clients about the appraisal process, and how you can best assist them. Two, what will it all cost? Just as the appraisal presentation and interaction with your client should be positive and professional, so should the manner in which fees are established and quoted.

A client who was confused about the fees charged, but paid them because of feeling obligated and committed to following through with the appraisal, will probably *not* be a repeat client. But more importantly, that client will carry a negative impression about appraisers, and possibly about jewelers. The keys once again: Specific quotes or estimates with a maximum, and no surprises.

## *Appraising can energize other aspects of your business*

It is obvious that a professional appraisal department can enhance a jeweler's image. As such services (provided by skilled, educated, conscientious, ethical appraisers) become more commonplace, appraisals will elevate the public's perception of our entire industry.

More so than when we sell jewelry or repair services, we take an aspect of the customer's life into our hands when we provide appraisal services. Financial decisions are made based upon appraisals—the need to make such decisions creates the need for appraisals.

Some very specific decisions might be based upon our insurance appraisals. What will be the maximum cash payout an insurance company will make in the event that an item is lost? How much will the premiums be, in order to implement the protection? Will the insurance company agree to insure the item in the first place? An underwriter may accept the appraisal in order to activate protection, and based upon that appraisal the upper limit of the insurance company's obligation to compensate for a loss will be established. But will a claims adjuster be clear about the nature and magnitude of a future loss, based upon the appraisal? All of these questions and more are involved in financial decisions that will be made based upon your appraisal.

If your appraisal results in a helpful, positive experience for your client immediately, when he or she purchases insurance, and in the future, when a loss occurs, you have energized your business by creating a relationship with someone who has truly been served—and knows it. You have had a positive effect on your client's life, and been paid for doing so. That client will tell other people about the positive experience, and in many cases will return to you for an important purchase, in which trust is a key element.

## *Staff Training:  Selling Appraisals = Selling Jewelry*

Many jewelers do not see the benefit in training staff to sell appraisal services. I believe that the more your staff knows about the appraisal process and the basis for the fees you charge, the more skilled they will be as salespeople.

It should be mentioned that the credibility of this argument is based upon one simple fact: Any store that offers appraisals should have a professional appraiser on staff. If you are the owner and do not think you can justify the expense and time away from your store, designate or hire someone else to do the job.

A professional appraiser is not simply someone who is knowledgeable about appraising. The professional also knows how to sell the service, and teach a store's staff how to do so. The professional appraiser may not have all the answers, but will know where to find them. This person will be articulate and literate. This professional will be skilled at emphasizing the value of your high-level appraisal services over those of the "handwritten-on-a-business form" appraisal.

The presence of such a person in a store will have a positive ripple effect. That appraiser will have insights into take-in procedures, many of which will carry over into your repair department. More comprehensive, orderly take-in procedures instill confidence in your customers. Sloppy take-in procedures, on the other hand, create doubt and concern and can lead to costly litigation.

The intelligent discussion of appraisal issues generates good will and confidence. It also opens the door to discuss the benefits of buying jewelry from an establishment that makes truthful disclosures in its documentation of the merchandise it sells. This is not to advise you to slander your competitors, nor is it meant to incite ill will between competing jewelers. But you paid for this book, and deserve to gain some practical knowledge that will make your investment worthwhile.

A note about selling appraisal services over the phone: The call that begins with, "How much do you charge for appraisals?" is problematic. If you begin your presentation by answering the question directly, you have a good chance of losing the job to someone who quoted lower. It is helpful, therefore, to sell the service before answering the question.

A good response might be, "Have you availed yourself of our appraisal services before?" If the answer is no, you have the opening you need to discuss the quality of your appraisal process. You can talk about your credentials, about the need for photographs and very detailed item descriptions if a loss occurs and the item is being replaced, and about your professionalism in general. Then you are ready to discuss your fee structure. If after you have made your presentation, the caller still wishes to continue shopping, you can bring out the heavy artillery.

It is a good idea to have a list of your credentials memorized or written down in a handy place. Even if these do not sink in during the initial presentation, you may have another opportunity to use them. Try this: "Madam, I understand that you would like to get the most for your money when you hire an appraiser. So I would like to give you some information that may be helpful in your search for an appraiser. I would suggest that you ask the following questions of any appraiser you are considering for this important service.

### Being Apprised of How Others Appraise

Many jewelers use overstated, inflated point-of-sale appraisals to make their competition look bad, or at the very least to demonstrate the bargain prices to be found in their stores. After all, if everything in Jeweler A's store is "worth" 50% more than it sells for, why would any reasonable consumer shop in Jeweler B's establishment? For example, let's say a jeweler in your area regularly appraises what he sells at 50% over his actual selling price. The $5,000.00 engagement ring is always "worth" $7,500.00. If you have a neighbor who operates this way, you may be losing diamond sales because your $5,000.00 engagement ring is only worth, well, $5,000.00.

Teaching your staff about appraisals will help them to combat the abuse of appraisals by those of your competitors who engage in such practices.

By properly educating your staff in the basics of appraisal ethics, you will create sales you might otherwise lose. Sometimes a simple question put to a customer, such as, "Don't you wonder how someone can afford to sell something for $5,000.00, if it's *worth* $7,500.00?" is enough to make the point. Other times a bit more may be required. One might explain to the customer that unless the discrepancy between selling price and appraised value is justified **in writing** as part of the appraisal, the appraisal is misleading.

1. Are your appraisals typewritten?
2. Do you include color photographs of my jewelry?
3. Do you draw plot diagrams of important diamonds?
4. Have you ever had your color vision and hue discrimination tested? [Note: Nearly everyone who is lucky enough to get this far in the affirmative will tumble here. Have *your* color vision and hue discrimination tested every three or four years—it is good business, good appraising, and helps to sell the service.]
5. Do you have any formal appraisal education? If so, tell me about it.
6. Are you a member of an appraisal society or association?
7. If so, are you credentialed or certified by that organization?
8. If you are, what were the requirements to achieve that designation?
9. Do you have formal gemological education?
10. Will I know in advance, exactly what the charges will be?

Of course, these questions are not necessarily the ones you will suggest. But obviously your list should conform quite closely to your own credentials. If you can answer all of your own questions in the affirmative, with solid explanations, one negative from your competitor could turn the customer back to you for the job. Be bold—this can be fun.

It is not uncommon for a potential appraisal customer, presented with a list similar to the one above, to simply decide that you must be qualified. This is not to suggest that you make up questions in the hope that you will not have to answer them yourself. Tailor the list to your qualifications, and watch the results. By formulating such a presentation, you are in essence asking the customer, "You would not ask a nurse to perform brain surgery, would you? So why entrust the appraisal that will lead to your important financial decision to someone who is unqualified?"

To editorialize for a moment, it is time that honest, ethical jewelers arm themselves with the intellectual ammunition provided by appraisal education and professional appraisal practices. An in-depth knowledge of appraisals will generate retail sales in your store. As stated in the foreword, education is the key. Perhaps the entire focus of the book is audacious in that sense. It assumes that you have availed yourself of some form of appraisal education already and will continue to update that knowledge, or that having read this book, you will seek to become an educated, true professional.

One person *can* make a difference. Thousands of clients, mine and those of other professional appraisers, have seen and experienced the difference between our appraisals and those pieces of paper merely called appraisals by the people who prepare them. Many if not most of those consumers have opportunities to refer their friends and colleagues to the establishments that practice a professional approach.

I will always remember the words of an attorney who had just concluded a major case involving the broker of some valuable property. The broker had abused his inherently conflicted dual role as both broker and appraiser, much to the detriment of the buyer. The attorney had worked closely with a professional appraiser. In reviewing the case during a lecture, the attorney commented that he had never had any idea just how much help an appraiser could be to an attorney, until he worked with this particular appraiser. The attorney fully believed that had it not been for this appraiser's thorough understanding of the appraisal process and insights into the manner in which the court would use the appraisal report, success in this case would not have been as easily attained, if attained at all. Powerful stuff, isn't it?

## Before you go on ...

This is a book about appraising jewelry for insurance purposes. Appraisals are widely understood in many professional communities to be unbiased, objective, informed opinions of value. These opinions should be based upon the realities of the marketplace where the items in question are commonly sold.

The jewelry industry has long accepted the jeweler's own point-of-sale insurance document as an appraisal. In fact, its lack of bias has to be questioned (when the seller is also the appraiser, can/will that jeweler be fair?). It may not be objective, since information deemed to be damaging to the sale or relationship may be omitted. Beyond the bias and objectivity issues, is value. One jeweler's selling price does not necessarily reflect common selling prices in the marketplace in general. Yet many jewelers have mistakenly accepted their selling prices as indicators of value.

Because this is a book about appraising, it must also cover the non-appraisal—that point-of-sale insurance document that is *not* truly an appraisal. This discussion does not preclude the jeweler's ability or right to provide these documents for customers. This value-added service is important to your business, and can be easy to generate. Chapter 2 discusses the concept in detail, and provides a sample form for implementation of the idea. The essence of the concept is this: Point-of-sale insurance documentation should restate the actual selling price unless a different dollar amount is justified. In those cases, the discrepancy between selling price and stated value (which in fact is not called value here, as you will see in Chapter 2) must be explained. Please continue to learn more about this significant issue.

# 2

*This Chapter does not Belong in this Book*

## Statement of Sale and Evaluation for Insurance

*"Okay Ralph, I'll put this chapter in the book...
but I'm telling you it doesn't belong."*

If you issue an appraisal for the jewelry you sell for an amount higher than the selling price, you may be putting your customers in jeopardy. In addition to the excess premiums which result, this can be legally treacherous, as you may be guiding your client toward failing to disclose a material fact to his or her insurance company. More about that later.

This chapter deals with the **Statement of Sale and Evaluation for Insurance**, also known generically as a point-of-sale insurance document, as an alternative to the appraisal as a means for retail jewelers to document their merchandise at the point of sale strictly for insurance use. It is important to note that the format discussed here is designed strictly for documentation of what you sell in your store. It is not recommended as a substitute for professional appraisals of outside merchandise, even if that merchandise is of a type that you regularly sell.

The jewelry industry has a big problem. That problem is the deliberate overstatement of value on jewelry appraisals (so called) that are prepared by many jewelers on their own merchandise at the point of sale. The appraisal profession has long been aware of this common jewelry industry practice. An appraisal by definition reflects market activity in general, not just within the seller's own place of business. This suggests that if we are employing only our own selling price irrespective of selling prices elsewhere, a document titled something *other* than an appraisal is appropriate.

The widespread practice of selling for one price and immediately appraising for another has thrived because the definition of appraisal is misunderstood by most consumers, and, to a much lesser extent, certain segments of the insurance industry. This lack of understanding explains consumers' acceptance of the word of jewelers who say, "I sell it for $5,000.00, but it would appraise for $8,000.00." The *Statement of Sale and Evaluation for Insurance* document helps to eliminate the *apparent* validity of that deceptive practice by stating very clearly that the retail replacement cost contained in the document is the same as the actual selling price, unless otherwise noted and explained.

The practice of overstatement causes problems from the beginning of the document's life cycle. Recently I spoke to an underwriting supervisor with a major insurance carrier. We discussed the issue of overstatement of value on point-of-sale insurance documents, and his response was interesting. "Well," he said, choosing his words carefully, "we just assume that any appraisal on new merchandise has a stated value higher than the selling price. We know that is the common practice, and we take it into account. If we found that a particular jeweler was not engaging in the practice of overstating value, we would have to treat that jeweler's point-of-sale insurance documentation differently." I found this shocking, even though I knew the problem existed. It means that this particular insurance company is willing to alter its entire system of establishing premiums and selling coverage, rather than demand the true selling price or explanation of the discrepancy between selling price and stated value. To continue with the thought, I also interpret this as indicating that the insurance industry sees the problem as hopeless, and may be taking on a "let them do their thing, and we'll do ours" attitude as a result. I would like to see the insurers working with our industry to control the practice of overstating value, rather than just adapting to it. Perhaps if enough of us provide insurers with honest, accurate insurance documents, that dialog will become a reality.

The beauty of using the *Statement of Sale and Evaluation for Insurance* document is that it clearly and simply defines itself: Ideally, consumers and insurance companies will know what it is, and what it is not. They will know when the stated retail replacement cost is the truth, and when it is not. This document's proper use illustrates your desire to deal honestly and fairly with your customers *and* insurance carriers, both of whom are victimized by *appraisals* which contain overstated values. [Note: within this chapter, when the word *appraisal* appears in italics, it refers to a point-of-sale document being improperly used as an appraisal.]  This document's improper use will be obvious, and hopefully will not be tolerated by the jewelry and insurance industries, or the public.  Its wording forces the user to either tell the truth, or... to very obviously **not** tell the truth.

### *Proper Use of the "Statement of Sale and Evaluation of Insurance" Document*

Proper use is essential if we are to maximize the format's positive effect on our industry.  Proper use includes a complete description of the item, a word picture such as that employed in a formal appraisal report.  The description should be sufficient to identify the item even without a photograph, although a photograph is an important addition which will enhance the document's effectiveness.  The more thorough the description, the better your customer's chance of receiving **"like kind and quality"** at the time of a loss, and the customer's opinion of you is enhanced forever.  Recommendations for a proper item description are discussed in detail in Chapter 8.

You have to exercise some common sense with regard to the choice of descriptive information dictated by the particular item.  For example, a cluster ring containing 20 commercial quality rubies would not call for descriptions of window and extinction in each gemstone.  However, the obvious requirements of estimated total weight, overall shape and cut, color, and clarity descriptions—essentially, statements about the overall quality of the rubies—are appropriate and necessary.

This chapter is meant to provide guidelines and recommendations for documenting what you sell, not binding rules.  This kind of documentation serves to protect your clients' right to have proper replacements, while treating insurance companies fairly by describing jewelry accurately and providing truthful statements of retail replacement prices in your store.

If an item is sold for $1,000.00, that figure should appear somewhere in the document.  It may be the same as the current retail price, unless the item regularly and truly sells for a higher price in your store.  If this is the case, the discrepancy should be disclosed and explained.  Tag (asking) prices do not necessarily constitute normal selling prices (i.e., gold chains which are always "50% off" in a particular store).

Following are three examples of point-of-sale insurance disclosures:

1. "This item is generally tagged and sold for $1,200.00 in this store; however, it was purchased on the date indicated during a restyling show, at a 20% discount, for $960.00.  The regular retail selling price in our store is $1,200.00, as stated, and numerous sales have been transacted on this item at that price.  It is therefore recommended that the item be insured for this amount."

2. "This item was purchased on the date indicated for $1,000.00.  On this occasion we extended a courtesy discount of $200.00 off our normal everyday selling price of $1,200.00.  The regular retail selling price in our store is $1,200.00 as stated, and numerous sales have been transacted at that price.  It is therefore recommended that the item be insured for this amount."

3. You carry a line of high-end watches.  This particular line is regularly discounted in your area, generally about 15% to 20% off of manufacturer's list (suggested retail) price.  You sell one of these watches, that has a manufacturer's suggested retail price of $10,000.00, for your usual selling price of $8,500.00.  With this kind of an item, where retail prices are published and generally known, it is appropriate to add a simple note to your document.  "This item has a manufacturer's list price of $10,000.00.  However, our everyday retail price [therefore, retail replacement cost in your store] is $8,500.00."  In this case, it is the perception of understated value which is being dealt with, rather than the opposite.

### *Flexibility*

The illustration that follows on pages 21 and 22 is a sample format for implementing the Statement of Sale and Evaluation for Insurance. Please examine that format before continuing. This document can easily be edited or enhanced in the following ways.

*1.* The ending statement which reads "We welcome inquiries about our professional appraisal services" obviously is not appropriate in all cases. It can be eliminated or revised based upon your own situation, needs, and qualifications.

*2.* Photographs and/or plot diagrams may be employed to enhance documentation when appropriate. These will most likely be added on a separate page unless there is room adjacent to the verbal description. I recommend highly that the document be paginated (i.e., Page 1 of 3, Page 2 of 3, etc.) in order to make the removal of any page(s) obvious to all concerned.

*3.* Tasteful cosmetic enhancement (using borders, logos, or other embellishment) will contribute to your store's image and professionalism.

*4.* You may want to attach a photocopy of your customer's sales slip to reinforce the integrity of the document.

### *Selling the idea to your customers*

Train yourself to illustrate the value of this document versus the traditional appraisal with which your customers are familiar. By definition, an appraisal reflects market activity and other elements which make it much more than simply a jeweler's subjective opinion of value, or simply the selling price in that jeweler's store.

It is important to illustrate that no one is served when a jeweler sells an item for one price on a daily basis, but consistently *appraises* at an inflated level, since this practice may result in problems later which are unforeseeable by your client now.

Your overstatement of value results in excess insurance premiums paid by your unsuspecting customer. In extreme cases, where large dollar amounts are involved, who is responsible for those wasted premiums? This is a question you should ask yourself before arbitrarily putting your client in the unenviable position of spending money unnecessarily on insurance premiums.

Your client is likely to be surprised, then dismayed, then angry when a loss occurs and he or she finds out that not only is the insurance company's cost of replacement below actual retail, it is also dramatically below the overstated *appraised* value.

### *One possible scenario you should avoid*

A simple example will illustrate further. You sell a diamond engagement ring for $15,000.00, *appraising* that ring for $22,000.00. A year later the ring is stolen, and an insurance claim is filed. The policy holder, your customer, files a claim, and through the insurance company's replacement vendor of choice, the company finds that it can replace the ring with one of "like kind and quality" for $12,000.00. When your customer states that she would like to have the cash rather than the replacement, she is informed that the cash settlement will be $12,000.00. "But I had the ring insured for $22,000!" she will exclaim.

The customer thinks she is entitled to the amount for which the item was insured. There may be legal implications as well. A lawsuit against the insurance company is likely to be

## STATEMENT OF SALE AND EVALUATION FOR INSURANCE

The item described below was purchased at this store on the date indicated, by or for the person(s) named below. Unless otherwise noted, the dollar amount stated is the actual price for which the item was sold (not overstated) and is also the retail price for which this establishment would replace it as of this date. This report may be used only to obtain insurance, and is not valid or defensible if used for other purposes.

**Prepared for:**
**Dr. and Mrs. Ross Stevens**
**918 Princeton Avenue**
**Harvard, New Jersey 08887**

**September 20, 1994**

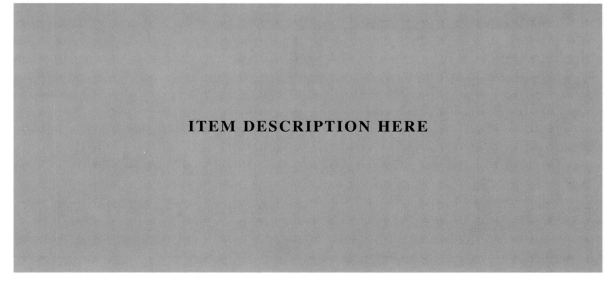

ITEM DESCRIPTION HERE

| | |
|---|---|
| **Current Retail Replacement Cost:** | **$1,000.00** |
| **Sales Tax @ 6%:** | **60.00** |
| **Total:** | **$1,060.00** |

_____

**Ralph S. Joseph**
**Graduate Gemologist (GIA)**

Because the item described herein was supplied by this establishment and the dollar amount stated reflects only OUR retail selling price, this document is NOT an appraisal. Its format is in keeping with our understanding that appraisals by definition are unbiased and reflect market research. We recommend to all insurers that any valuation document which is prepared at the point of sale and entitled "APPRAISAL" be verified as containing _actual selling price_, rather than an overstated, arbitrary value statement. We welcome inquiries about our professional appraisal services.

# SAMPLE
[REVERSE SIDE OF FORM]

## Use of the "Statement of Sale and Evaluation for Insurance"

The "Statement of Sale and Evaluation for Insurance" is a suggested alternative for jewelers who are justifiably uncomfortable with "appraising" the merchandise they sell. This format is designed strictly for insurance documentation, with the stated retail price to be used by insurance companies as the basis for premiums. Any other use of this format voids the document, and such misuse is likely to mislead a third party user.

An appraisal should be impartially prepared by a disinterested (unbiased) party, and should set forth a qualified opinion of value which is supported by market data. Therefore a document prepared at the point-of-sale, for insurance purposes, is technically not an "appraisal." Such documents generally do not reflect the market beyond the jeweler's own store, and the seller of an item is not impartial. The "Statement of Sale and Evaluation for Insurance" specifically dictates that the stated replacement price is that at which the preparer/jeweler sold the item in his/her store. When the selling price and stated "Retail Replacement Cost " (or "price") differ, an explanation will be provided. Without such explanation this document is not valid.

### Important Note to Consumers
Do not allow the issuing jeweler to overstate the retail replacement price of the item described in this document unless the discrepancy is clearly explained. The practice of overstating value may create a "moral hazard" and as a consequence result in a voided insurance claim! Overstatement of selling price or value does not serve you.

### What the "Statement of Sale and Evaluation for Insurance" Should Contain

This document should contain an item description sufficient to properly identify the item and to replace it with one of "like kind and quality" in the event of a loss. A certain level of gemological competence is required for the preparation of this document. The preparer, if not Graduate Gemologist (GIA) or Fellow of the Gemmological Association of Great Britain (FGA), should at the very least have formal gemological education related to the type of jewelry being documented (i.e., completion of the Gemological Institute of America's "Diamonds" and "Diamond Grading" courses if documenting diamond jewelry), or secure the assistance of another member of the jeweler's staff who does possess that knowledge. Because most insurance policies cover replacement with "like kind and quality," **detailed descriptions are essential.** Such descriptions will enhance the insurance company's ability to meet this obligation.

*NOTE TO READERS: None of the information contained in this instructional document should be construed as the dispensing of legal advice. It is copyrighted material, developed to illustrate a concept for documenting merchandise at the point-of-sale.*
   *An attorney should be consulted before relying on any of the material contained here.*

unsuccessful because of the manner in which insurers promise to cover losses. Most insurance policies contain wording similar to the following:

"Unless otherwise stated in this policy, covered property values will be determined at the time of the loss or damage occurrence. We will pay the cost of repair or replacement, not to exceed the smallest of the following amounts: a) the full amount of our cost to repair the property to its condition immediately prior to the loss or damage occurrence; b) the full amount of our cost to replace the item with one substantially identical to the item lost or damaged (sometimes known as "like kind and quality"); c) any special limit of liability described in this policy, or d) the limit of liability applicable to the property." Please note "not to exceed the smallest of the following amounts."

This underscores the importance of stating value (or your selling price, in this case) accurately. Overstating an item's cost of replacement benefits no one, and might harm your customer.

In a case where an insured sued an insurance company when the company refused to pay on a burglary claim, a circuit court in Illinois found the following: "Insured's failure to disclose on application for insurance coverage of art objects at their appraised value that the same dealer who sold him objects for $19,800.00 contemporaneously appraised the objects at $275,800.00 constituted misrepresentation that materially affected insurer's risk and furnished grounds for rescission of Insurance coverage." [Stone v. Those Certain Underwriters at Lloyd's 481 N.E. 2d 422].

The Illinois court found in favor of the insurance company by rescinding the insurance coverage on the objects. The insured's failure to disclose the discrepancy between the cost of the objects and the amount for which they were insured furnished grounds for rescission of the insurance coverage. The court found that "the failure to reveal such facts prevented the defendant [insurance company] from appraising the risk as it actually existed ... this case is not concerned with an instance where a misleading statement was made, rather it involves plaintiff's failure to disclose information." Asked one appraiser, "If you were Stone, wouldn't you sue the appraiser?"

### *Another possible scenario to avoid (previously described by William Hoefer in "The Guide")*

You sell a one carat diamond solitaire engagement ring to Ms. Sueya. You sell it for $5,000, and write a point-of-sale *appraisal* stating a value of $7,500.00. Six months later, the diamond is lost from its mounting. Ms. Sueya blames *you*, and demands that you replace the diamond at no cost to her. You can see that the ring has been abused, and refuse to replace the diamond. Ms. Sueya, well, sues you. The court determines that the ring was defective, and decides in her favor; now it is time to determine the award. You have three choices. You can pay the $7,500.00 judgment. After all, you are the one who said the diamond was worth that. Or, you can state in court that you are not really qualified to appraise, and therefore the $7,500.00 is bogus. Or, you can state in court that you purposely misrepresented the value of the diamond. No matter what, you look bad. The important thing is, if you say the diamond is worth $7,500.00 and your customer makes a financial decision because of her reliance on your expertise, a court of law is likely to agree with you on the value, much to your detriment. There is also the possibility that an angry client will sue you to recover excess premiums paid based upon your overstated value.

### *Know the laws in your state and protect yourself and your customers*

Not to bore you with this subject, but to drive the point home: Failure by an insured to disclose material facts, such as the seller/appraiser are the same person, and/or overstated value is in dramatic excess of the selling price, can cause serious problems. Most insurance applications contain a question such as, "Is there any other material fact regarding this proposal of insurance which should be made known to the Insurance Company for consideration?" This wording obligates your customer to disclose at the inception of the policy the fact that you are the seller, and that your stated value exceeds the selling price. Failure on the part of your customer to make this disclosure could result in the denial of a future claim. When your customer's claim is denied and that denial is upheld in court via a vacated claim, whereby premiums are returned and the insurance company is not required to pay the claim, the next step could be a successful subsequent lawsuit against the jeweler/appraiser: you.

In most states, insurance policies include a condition which states that the entire policy shall be void if, whether before or after the loss, the insured willfully conceals or misrepresents any material fact concerning the insurance. In the state of New York, the insurance code makes the insurance company pay the claim; the insurance company can then sue the consumer and participating parties (often the appraiser). The laws regarding valuation policy vary from state to state. Make sure that you become familiar with the laws in your state so that you do not inadvertently put yourself or your customers at risk. Enough said.

---

Now you have a clear picture of the difference between an appraisal and a point-of-sale insurance document — the *Statement of Sale and Evaluation for Insurance*. As stated already in many ways, this particular document is not an appraisal. However, what is described in the remaining chapters of this book most certainly *is* an appraisal. The differences will continue to become abundantly clear.

# 3

*The Big Bad Wolf, or Little Red Riding Hood?*

## A Few Words About
## Insurance Companies

There has been considerable debate, on the Polygon® computer network and elsewhere, about who is at fault when an insurance company accepts a poor appraisal. Some argue that as long as the insurance industry accepts inadequate appraisals, the jewelry industry has no obligation to improve the quality of the appraisal product. The other side of the argument says that as professionals, we are obligated to our clients to do the job correctly, independently of insurance industry standards. While both arguments make sense, the truth probably lies with a combination of the two.

The insurance industry must bear some responsibility for having few, and in some cases, almost no standards at all on the underwriting level for jewelry. Handwritten, two-line appraisals for $5,000.00 items, complete with misspellings and fuzzy or non-existent details, are routinely accepted, and risk is underwritten based upon these inadequate appraisals. One insurance company executive on the West Coast has been quoted as saying, "I don't want my people to recognize a good appraisal. As things stand now, jewelry insurance is a big profit center for our company." A survey of one company determined that well over half of its agents in a particular state did not know how jewelry claims are processed and settled when a loss occurs.

## "Hey, He Was Asking For It."

The common argument that the insurance industry deserves inadequate appraisals because it does not demand more, sounds good on the surface. Certainly it rationalizes poor performance by an appraiser. This reasoning can be compared to other faulty logic.

A man opens his wallet to pay the tab at a nice restaurant. In doing so he exposes a large amount of cash. He is mugged and robbed outside the restaurant as he approaches his car. Does he bear some responsibility for not being more careful by concealing his money? Perhaps. But does this justify the actions of the mugger? Of course not.

The insurance industry accepts poor appraisals on a regular basis. If jewelers know this, and take advantage of the opportunity to skimp on their appraisals they damage their customers and the insurance companies. Is this any more justifiable than the mugging?

As appraisers, we have to exercise the same self control and discipline that are the hallmarks of a civilized society. Good behavior — our appraisal practices — should be determined by our pride in our work, dedication to professionalism, and the desire to do what is right. We should not be mugging the insurance companies. The jewelry industry does not need the insurance industry to establish its level of professionalism. That is up to us.

Dealings with claims representatives (adjusters) can easily arouse the public's disdain for the underwriting process. After the fact, when a loss has occurred, the adjuster must often inform the insured that there is insufficient detail contained in the appraisal, and that accurate replacement will therefore be difficult to accomplish. Imagine being that policy holder, having paid premiums for years, then being told that settling the claim will be difficult. One of two things will happen. Either the replacement item will exceed the quality of the original piece (a possibility that works to the policy holder's advantage), or it will be a replacement that will suffice, because the confused policy holder has no choice but to accept it or a *cash out.* Unfortunately for the insurance industry, the former scenario is all too common.

The disadvantage of the cash out, particularly in this situation, is that generally it will not be for the full insured amount. Many jewelry consumers function under the false assumption that a higher appraised value results in a higher cash settlement when a loss occurs. This is absolutely not true, of course, when the policy calls for replacement with "like kind and quality." The cash settlement is determined in these cases strictly according to the insurance company's actual cost to replace the item. Even if the cash out is for the full insured amount, the policy holder is now on his or her own, trying to navigate the waters of jewelry replacement without the assistance of the adjuster and the insurance company's trusted replacement sources.

Certainly the insurance industry has to bear some responsibility for this appalling state of affairs. Perhaps its lack of reaction is a sign of complacency. Or maybe the executive on the West Coast speaks for a certain segment of the industry. Whatever the insurance industry's position, as appraisers, we have a moral and ethical—a professional—responsibility to serve our clients to the best of our ability, regardless of the lesser requirements imposed by third party users of our appraisals.

Although this book was written primarily for jewelers, the insurance industry is addressed here. By raising underwriting requirements and standards as an industry, insurers can improve their images, and ultimately make life easier for policy holders who sustain a loss. After all, an unhappy policy holder is just as likely (perhaps more likely) to blame the insurance company as they are the appraiser.

## Flawed Gemology

A jeweler sold a one carat diamond and provided a point of sale insurance "appraisal," which stated that the diamond was G color and $VS_1$ clarity. Over the years the same jeweler updated his own appraisal several times. In the late 1980's, he had occasion to do so once again. This time, however, he graded the diamond D color, Internally Flawless, and valued it at $40,000. This price was high for the diamond at the time, even assuming that the new grading had been accurate.

The underwriter at the insurance company that had insured the ring all along, passed the new appraisal through, and coverage was secured.

Several months later the woman who owned the ring died, and her husband gave the ring to his daughter-in-law (his deceased wife's daughter). She took the recent appraisal to *her* insurance company, but it was not accepted because it was more than six months old, and had another individual's name on it.

At the time the ring had been given to the daughter-in-law, she had immediately taken it to the jeweler who had sold and continually appraised it, to have it sized.

During the time between this sizing and the insurance company's refusal to accept the appraisal, the jeweler had gone out of business and was therefore not available to re-appraise the ring. The woman decided to take the ring elsewhere for appraisal. The new appraisal declared that the diamond was J color, and $SI_1$ clarity.

The first owner (the father-in-law) concluded that the out-of-business jeweler (who, by the way had also declared business and personal bankruptcy) must have switched the diamond when he had sized it several months before. He filed a claim with his insurance company, who still had it covered as a D color, Internally Flawless, $40,000.00 diamond. The question was, would they cover it as such and pay on the claim?

Obviously the underwriter had not done his job, having overlooked the substantial upgrade in the diamond's stated quality. The diamond's original owner appeared to be trying to take advantage of that situation. The case settled out of court, and the results of the settlement were not made known to the public.

Many insurance carriers sell their products through agents. These companies have a problem that companies selling directly to the public do not have. Imagine an underwriter who decides to tighten up standards on his own. He begins rejecting appraisals that do not contain sufficient information or detail, and also goes a step further and demands a photograph of each item. The appraisal goes back to the agent with a note explaining the requirements, and the agent informs his client (perhaps a new client) that they will have to secure another appraisal. This one will probably cost some money, whereas the first most likely did not if it was provided by the seller. "Well, my old company never made me spend money for an appraisal. I guess I'll just stay with them!" is the reply that the agent does not want to hear. So, do agents put subtle pressure on underwriters to push appraisals through? Is collecting the premium more important than protecting the client? These questions have been asked time and time again by frustrated jewelers and, in a quiet way, by some people in the insurance industry. These questions, however, can only be answered by individuals involved in these scenarios. As appraisers, we can ask questions, but our obligation to perform professionally does not change.

I have never heard of an appraisal being rejected by an underwriter because it was *too* good. So there is no reason, short of ignorance or laziness, to skimp on the quality of a document that might become very important to your customer. Do the job right, and everyone wins— including, in the long run, the insurance company.

There is another element of this discussion that bears examination. One underwriting manager on the East Coast told me that his underwriters assume that the stated value on an insurance appraisal written by the jeweler who sold the item is overstated. This assumption gives his department a cushion, which makes replacement easier, but of course costs the insured extra premiums.

When I informed this manager that my appraisals were specifically designed to generate accurate replacement without requiring wasted premiums, he was genuinely surprised. I explained that items in my store were appraised at the point of sale not for an inflated, over-stated, arbitrary value, but for the restated selling price. "If you are telling the truth and that is really the case," he exclaimed, "then we will have to rethink our underwriting policies when we see point-of-sale appraisals that come from your establishment."

So if this manager's perception is correct, the insurance industry has trained itself to respond to appraisals which are prepared not objectively, but subjectively, with value state-ments that serve the jeweler's need to inflate value in the mind of the consumer. By inflating values, jewelers have therefore laid the groundwork for a frustrated insurance industry to respond by setting up a system whereby insurance companies ultimately profit. Translated into millions of consumers and many millions or even billions of premium dollars, this situa-tion is appalling.

To some, it may seem that the insurance companies' premiums are artificially high. After all, an item properly appraised at $5,000.00 might very well be replaced by an insurance company at a cost of $4,000.00. Isn't that unfair? No, because premiums are based upon the insurer's statistical data regarding losses, both in the percentage of policy holders that sustain losses and in dollars in particular categories. Part of the calculating process is the under-standing that insurance companies do not pay the full retail prices charged to private consumers.

A letter to the editor of one jewelry industry magazine suggested that we all appraise jewelry for the amount that an insurance company would pay. This, however, is faulty logic. Because if insurers consistently have to pay 100 percent of appraised value when the policy calls for replacement "at our cost," premiums will naturally go up. To repeat, the premium is set with the knowledge that if the appraisal contains an accurate retail replacement value/cost, the insurer will be able to purchase it for less. Insurance companies are volume buyers, there-fore they are justifiably big discount buyers. As I have told many customers while working on a claim, "If *you* buy one hundred items a year from us, you can buy for the same price the insurance company pays." This generally makes the point. Just as we do our customers no favor by overstating value, we do not serve them by understating value, thereby risking inade-quate monetary coverage, and ultimately contributing to a rise in premiums. Conservatism in estimating value is generally a good practice when replacement policies are involved. Many insurance underwriters actually favor this practice, as it protects their policy holders without causing undue premium expense.

It has been suggested that we include two values in all of our insurance appraisals. Appraisers are obligated, according to this argument, to disclose the fact that insurers pay less than retail, and to include the actual price that will be paid by them if a loss occurs. It is a good idea to include a statement in your AID (please see Chapters 7 and 8) that "insurance companies are volume buyers, therefore discount buyers, which may result in a cash settlement offer that is less than the retail replacement value stated in the appraisal." This provides valuable information for your client, and might prevent an uncomfortable surprise if a loss does occur.

However, I think that to quote the insurance company's actual cost of replacement is impractical and unnecessary. The insurance company's cost of replacement is difficult if not impossible to track. We have no way of following the specific vendors employed by insurers as replacement sources. In fact, these sources are generally confidential. Additionally, each replacement source has its own pricing structure, and in fact might have a set commission structure with certain companies. The prices paid are too inconsistent, and tracking them does not seem to be the job of the appraiser. To repeat however, it is a good idea to inform your customer that a cash settlement offer is likely to be less than the insured amount. This entire discussion becomes moot of course, when we are dealing with the *"agreed value"* policy that pays the insured amount in cash at the time of the loss.

As for insurance agents, they can be good, bad, or indifferent, just as in any other profession. I would challenge agents to, at the very least, seek out qualified appraisers to whom they can refer their valued clients. A list of at least three local appraisers will allow consumers to make their own choice, rather than an agent risking the fallout of sending a client to a particular appraiser and having the client dissatisfied with the referral. An understanding of the basics of appraising would be helpful, and hopefully this book will find its way into the hands of some agents (hint, hint, insurance companies!). Beyond that, insurance agents would be wise to focus on what is best for their clients. If a poorly prepared appraisal does not serve the client, an agent who points this out will be appreciated.

Be mindful of the fact that the insurance company and the appraiser have something in common—the client. It is unprofessional and impolite for appraisers to disparage insurance companies in discussions with clients. This serves no useful purpose, and creates bad feelings toward both parties. It is helpful to have a general discussion about claims settlement, in order to alert your clients to the importance of shopping for the coverage that suits them best. We are not insurance experts and should not hold ourselves out as such. But an appropriately timed, cursory introduction to the world of jewelry insurance replacement will be appreciated.

In conclusion, the ethical responsibility for properly prepared appraisals is the appraiser's. We cannot repair the insurance industry. We can only do our job correctly, and hope that other disciplines will follow suit. After all, we have contributed to the negative spiral of inadequate replacements and inflated premiums. Perhaps excellence can be just as contagious.

# 4

*Up Periscope*

## The Role of Gemology in Appraising

The common rallying cry of the jeweler not formally versed in professional appraising has long been, "Sure I'm an appraiser. I studied gemology at GIA." The average consumer makes the same assumption. "I need some things appraised. Do you have a gemologist on staff?" is a common question. Though the role of gemology in appraising cannot be ignored, it is fair to say that if gemology equals appraisal knowledge, this book would not have been worth writing. And please do not tell me that!

So what role does gemology play in the processes discussed throughout this book? Must one be a gemologist to be an appraiser of gems and jewelry? Technically, no. As one appraisal educator says, "You do not have to be a gemologist to appraise jewelry, any more than you have to be a metallurgist. Nor must you be a chemist to appraise oil paintings!" Again, technically these statements are true.

### Up Periscope

An independent appraiser (call him Jeff) on the West Coast received a telephone call from a frantic jeweler client. "Jeff," the jeweler said, "I need to make an appointment with you for this afternoon. It's really important!" Jeff replied, "Slow down a minute, what's so pressing?" The jeweler continued, "Well, I've got this gemstone I have to identify right away, and I need you to meet me down at the harbor, where that submarine is docked." His curiosity aroused, Jeff responded, "Okay, I can see you this afternoon, but why on the submarine?" "Because someone told me that to positively identify this gemstone, I have to subject it to a periscope test." After he stopped laughing, Jeff told the jeweler that the word was *polariscope*, and made the appointment to test the gem.

An appraiser who is truly well versed in the ethics, methodology, and thought processes required for professional appraising might very well hire a gemologist to handle gem identification and quality analysis, and possibly even value research. As long as the appraisal discloses that the appraiser and the identifier/authenticator are not the same person, and assuming of course that the information provided is accurate, this is perfectly acceptable. Of course it is a tremendous convenience to the appraiser to be able to perform most if not all of his or her own gemological work. But it is not essential.

Let us carry the example of the art appraiser a bit further. Our appraiser is asked to appraise a 19th century oil painting. The appraiser is aware that many fakes of this particular artist's work were created in the 1940s. However, the detection can be made by analyzing the pigment in the paint. If it contains a chemical that was not in existence in the 19th century, the painting would be positively identified as a fake. So, does our appraiser have to be a chemist in order to appraise the painting? Of course not. He simply obtains a chemist's analysis of the paint pigment, includes any pertinent written information in the appraisal, and identifies the chemist. He can then proceed with his identification and authentication, complete his research, and render the appraisal report.

One important point to be made about gemology is that there is nothing

### I've Heard the Term "Pigeon's Blood Ruby," but...

A gem dealer who was set up in Tucson one year reported an unusual shopper who visited his booth. The gentleman was looking for fine rubies.

One particular gem caught his eye, and he was moving it from one light source to another, and looking at from every direction. Still not satisfied, but very interested in the ruby, he performed an unusual color comparison test.

He removed his identification badge, stabbed his finger with the pin, squeezed some blood out of the wound, and proceeded to compare the ruby to the color of his own blood!

to be gained by trying to fool clients or other users of our appraisals. If you are not gemologically competent to perform a particular identification or grading procedure, simply hire someone who is and note that participation in the report. If you put gemological information in writing, it is critical that you be able to justify and explain it. One way of doing that is by having the gemological expertise, and saying so in your appraisal. The other, of course, is to explain that an outside expert was retained to perform the particular task. In the latter case, if the gemological work is ever questioned, you can properly attribute the work to the outside expert, and bring that expert in to explain the work or even testify as to the nature and results of that work.

The question is often asked, "How much gemological knowledge do I really need to be an appraiser?" Again, the answer is technically, "None at all." As a matter of practical convenience, that answer does not suffice. Depending upon the amount and kind of appraisal work you plan to engage in, the answer varies. Some appraisers concentrate heavily on appraisal principles and procedures, to the detriment of their gemological development. To repeat again, that is acceptable, as long as they know what their limitations are, adapt to them, and disclose them. One well-known appraiser once noted during a lecture, "I am a mediocre gemologist because I have spent a great deal of my time studying the science of appraising. My gemological skills are adequate for nearly every assignment that comes my way. But when something is out of my league gemologically, I refer it elsewhere or hire a more qualified gemologist to assist me."

## Gemology ≠ Appraising

A California jeweler was put on the spot when a long-time customer asked him to make an offer to purchase a diamond ring. The ring consisted of a domed top with six diamonds, five surrounding a slightly larger center diamond. The total weight in round, modern brilliant diamonds, approximately H to I color and SI clarity, was 1.50 carats. The ring was saleable, but not distinctive.

The jeweler made what he thought was a reasonable but "soft" offer, explaining that he was not particularly interested because of the generic nature of the ring. The customer began to leave the store in a foul mood, after declaring that he had been told by someone else that the ring would retail for $12,000.00. When asked who had made that value statement, and what qualified him to do so, the customer replied, "He said he was qualified...he told me he's a gemologist."

There are two lessons here. The first is that gemology and appraising are two different disciplines. The second is that verbal appraisals are particularly volatile because of the "he said, she said" syndrome they may be subjected to.

The jeweler was unable to console the customer, who adopted a "you're trying to rip me off" attitude and never returned to the store.

As merchants and, ultimately, appraisers, how much can we rely on our suppliers for gemological information about the products we purchase from them? Hoping not to offend any supplier, it is recommended that you err on the side of caution when making any representation about gems that you sell. Suppliers can make mistakes. Even the most honest suppliers may not double check on *their* suppliers. In our store, for example, we like to check every diamond that we purchase to verify the color and clarity represented. And no laboratory should be sacred in that regard. It is a good habit to check reports, even the GIA's diamond grading reports, despite their reputation for objectivity and consistency. You may disagree, and if so, it is acceptable, even critical, to say so in your appraisal. When you are in agreement with the report (which in actual practice is nearly always), include a statement such as "This diamond is accompanied by GIA/GTL (or other lab's) Diamond Grading Report #123456, dated 1/11/96, stating that the diamond weighs 1.10 carats, and is H color and VS$_1$

clarity. The undersigned has examined the diamond, determined that it is the same as that described in the report, and agrees with the color and clarity assigned. Other information is contained in the report, a copy of which is included as Page 6 of this appraisal. The stated estimate of value is based upon the assumption that the information in the lab report is correct." Included in such a statement, it is advisable also to refer the user back to your AID, in the section that discusses the subjectivity of diamond grading. Tailor the statement to your own needs and the reality of the particular situation, but include something of an explanatory nature. You will find that your clients will appreciate the effort you made to verify the information in the lab report.

Some appraisers resort to vague or incomplete gemological information, with the mistaken belief that nobody really cares. The bad news (well, good news if you are serious about the subject) is that somebody *does* care. Insurance companies, to be sure, are interested in correct and complete gemological information. There are exceptions, but in the end the lack of information will turn insurance adjusters and underwriters against the offending appraisers. One claims adjuster in New Jersey refuses to speak to one particular jeweler because of his reputation for "fudging" or simply omitting information on appraisals. This means the jeweler is missing out not only on more appraisal business (and who cares about that, right?), but also potential insurance replacement work that can be quite lucrative. The bottom line is, include the information if you have it, and if you do not have it, get it—*then* include it!

Some firms have their own grading systems for diamonds. A gemologist/appraiser once told me a disturbing story. The store he worked for, part of a large chain, asked him to revise its grading system to make it compare more favorably with the GIA system. The gemologist refused to take on the task, for obvious ethical reasons. He was not terminated from his

### Don't shoot me, I'm just the gemologist!

A customer with a reputation for "harmless volatility" came into my store with a ring that contained a broken green stone. She wanted it identified. This was prior to my gemological studies, yet it was obvious from the nature of the break and other characteristics of the stone that it was glass. The customer was not convinced that my immediate assessment was correct. She insisted that I check further, because she was certain that she was in possession of an emerald.

To appease her and avoid a scene in front of an ever-building group of customers, I took a token glance at the gem under the microscope. I repeated my earlier identification, but the customer continued to insist that it was an emerald. I asked her to please wait until I had taken care of some other customers, if she wished to discuss the matter further. Not to be placed in a secondary position, she continued to talk about her "emerald" to any-

one who would listen.

I heard a voice say, "Excuse me, I think I can help. I'm a gemologist." I looked up to see a man in his twenties, nicely dressed and well groomed. He came forward to the counter, and the customer looked at him excitedly. "Thank goodness," she said, "someone who knows what he's doing!" Embarrassed at being upstaged by someone who might know more than I did, I assured the young man that I could handle the situation. "No, I insist," he said. "I'm a gemologist."

He took the ring from the woman, looked at it very closely, and said, "Aha, I know just what this is." "Yes, well what is it?" the anxious customer queried. "This," he exclaimed, "is a Jujube!" The now angry woman grabbed the ring and stormed out of the store. "Are you really a gemologist?" I asked. "Oh, of course not," he replied, "I just got tired of waiting my turn!"

position, but another employee was engaged to do the work, and our honest friend never felt comfortable at his job after the incident.

Even if you have created your own diamond grading system with integrity, it can cause problems if it is not explained.  It is advisable to include some explanation, or at the very least make one available, of any system you use— including the GIA system.  If you assume that consumers know nothing about what you do as an appraiser, you will find yourself many steps ahead of your competition in the eyes of your appraisal clients.

## About enhancements

In the context of appraising, gemstone enhancements are important, just as they are in retailing in general.  In retailing there is a long-standing discussion about what treatments and enhancements should be disclosed.  Some argue that if a treatment is commonly accepted in the trade (i.e., heat-treating blue sapphires or oiling emeralds), it need not be disclosed.  My only comment is, try telling that to the customer who has that sapphire identified by a gemologist or independent laboratory as "heat-treated," and see whether or not disclosure is important!  You will be asked in no uncertain terms why you did not inform the purchaser of this aspect of the gemstone.  Failure to disclose *any* fact considered important in the buyer's decision about whether to make a purchase could result in a successful claim of fraud.

As appraisers, it is important that we provide information that might be useful to the owner of the jewelry, and to third parties who rely on our work.  One appraiser simply encloses an extensive glossary of gemstone treatments with every appraisal.  When asked why he does not simply provide information on the pertinent gems, he replied, "If I single out the specific gem (i.e., the sapphire appears to be heat treated), the client has a tendency to panic, as though there is an urgency about the disclosure and perhaps a reason to worry about the gemstone.  But by providing the entire list, the client is assured that many, if not most, gems are enhanced in some way, and the information about their particular gem is taken in a healthier context.  This is better for the client, and for the jeweler through whom the assignment was secured."

Some treatments may be less common, and not necessarily included on even an extensive list.  Fracture filling has become common, particularly in diamonds.  However, emeralds are fracture

### The Emperor's New Disclosure

Several appraisers attended a talk given by renowned gemologist Kurt Nassau during an appraisal conference in New Orleans.  Mr. Nassau was discussing irradiation of topaz and the ramifications of the treatment, including the fact that at one time radioactive material was being imported into the United States.

Their curiosity aroused, a few of the appraisers decided to go "shopping," to find out what kind of disclosures were being made of this particular treatment.  One stop was in a very fine, upscale store.  After asking to see a blue topaz bracelet, one of the gemologists asked the salesperson about the radiation used to generate blue color in topaz.

The salesperson informed the group that in fact, irradiation of blue topaz had ceased in the 1940's "because it was killing people," and that all of the blue topaz in this store was absolutely, naturally blue.

Of the six or seven stores visited by this group of gemologists, the only one that disclosed the use of radiation to treat blue topaz was a pawn shop that carried quite a bit of the material.

filled with increasing frequency, and there may be experimentation with other gemstones as well.  These enhancements certainly bear discussion in the appraisal, independent of the glossary of treatments that you might include with your appraisal.  A good rule is as follows:  If the enhancement is so common that it is a part of the market for the gem in question and untreated gems sell for the same price, a separate discussion may not be necessary.  If the treatment has a definite effect upon value or replacement value and cost, it should be discussed separately and thoroughly.

Fracture filled diamonds are a good example. A fracture filled diamond that is, for example, H color and SI$_2$ clarity, might very well have been G/I$_2$ prior to treatment. This means, of course, that it was purchased at the G/I$_2$ price, then treated for a minimal fee, and sold at an appropriate price (assuming the integrity of merchants at all levels along the way). Some laboratories will not even grade fracture filled diamonds, preferring simply to reject them and return them to the submitting party. The logic of the practice is that the diamond's apparent clarity and possibly color have been altered by the enhancement process, therefore one cannot know what its grades are, and cannot provide a laboratory report.

As of this writing, the GIA/GTL laboratory will not provide grading reports for fracture filled diamonds. In that sense, use of the GIA diamond grading terminology actually makes the appraisal hypothetical. If GIA will not assign a grade for a fracture filled diamond, and you use their nomenclature to describe one, the appraisal should contain an explanation. A statement such as, "The use of GIA diamond grading terminology implies that the GIA Gem Trade Laboratory would assign a similar grade, or a different grade using the same nomenclature. Please be advised that at this time, the GIA laboratory will *not* assign any grade to fracture filled diamonds." This removes the illusion that your grade is somehow a "GIA grade," as the public often thinks it is. Your AID should also make clear that this is your opinion of a diamond's grade (not just fracture filled, but any diamond), and that you employ GIA's nomenclature, not its system or procedures. Unless you have worked in GIA's laboratory, and actually employ their system and methodology, make it clear that you use only their nomenclature.

If, as an appraiser, you choose to provide the service on a fracture filled diamond, be sure to carefully explain the ramifications of the enhancement. You should disclose the severe limitations upon your ability to discern what grades the diamond might have displayed prior to being fracture filled. In fact, you may not be concerned at all about how the diamond looked prior to the enhancement. More about that in a moment. Explain the methodology you are using to estimate replacement cost. If you are assuming a particular original grade or grades, then adding the cost of treatment and an appropriate markup to determine retail cost, then by all means discuss your logic in the appraisal. But this methodology is suspect. The reality is that the diamond appears as it appears, and has a selling price in the marketplace similar to other diamonds that have similar appearance. Research of actual transactions in fracture filled diamonds will reveal the most accurate valuation data. Find out what fractured filled diamonds similar to your subject diamond sell for, and you will know about what it is worth.

Additional information should be provided. Define the enhancement. For example, "Fracture filling is a process whereby, under tremendous heat and pressure, a glass-like substance is infused into any surface-reaching inclusions in the diamond, thereby making them less visible both to the naked eye and under magnification. The effect upon the diamond's weight has been determined in studies to be infinitesimal. Color grades may decrease by one to two grades or not at all, and apparent clarity may increase by one to three grades."

Stability issues should also be addressed. For example: "Fracture filling compounds are generally stable under normal usage. However, some tests indicate that certain filling materials may become tinted yellow with time and exposure to certain kinds of light or other conditions. Additionally, the heat required to repair or retip a prong, for example, is sufficient to melt or otherwise damage the filling material, thereby temporarily destroying the enhanced appearance of your diamond. Generally, damaged fracture filling

**Now don't get irritated ...**

A jewelry lover on the West Coast was treated to an unusual education in a local retail store. She asked how mabe pearls were formed. "Well," the salesperson responded, "the oyster is subjected to an irritant. Then, instead of creating a regular kind of pearl, it just goes 'poof!'"

can be removed entirely, and the diamond retreated with no damaging effect to the diamond itself. It is recommended that you contact the jeweler from whom you purchased the diamond, the manufacturer who treated the diamond, or both, in order to gain further knowledge of the process and its ultimate durability."

By providing the information suggested here, you will have fulfilled a basic but critical obligation to your appraisal client. The statements above in quotes are adequate for appraisal purposes, and certainly alert the diamond's owner that the enhancement is not ordinary, and could bear further investigation.

As stated throughout this book, a good way to remember to provide enhancement information is to follow this simple rule: Think about what you're doing, do it, then explain what you have done—in writing, in the appraisal report.

# 5 *So What is it Worth?*

## Arriving at a Reasonable Estimate of Value

N o matter how much information jewelers have about formats, technology, and logistics, one question is still commonly asked of appraisal educators and writers. "How much markup do you put on things?" is the recurring theme, if not the precise question. As with most of appraising, the answer is not simple, but it is logical. It also has to be expanded to be answered correctly. So, one thing at a time.

### Use vs. Misuse of Price Guides

There has been much debate in the appraisal profession about the proper use of price guides and lists. They are different, and may have different ramifications in your appraisal work. For the purposes of this discussion, I would classify a **price guide** as a compilation of research materials, assembled in order to give price indications for certain kinds of products. Gemworld International's *The Guide* is a good example. Enormous amounts of research and input from gemstone sources are compiled to provide ranges of wholesale, memo selling prices for various gem materials. A **price list** is just that—a list of items for sale, with the prices being asked for them on a particular basis (i.e., memo, cash, net 30 days, etc.).

The first criterion for their use is the determination that they are accurate. If you plan to use a price guide as a research tool in your appraising, try comparing its prices to actual purchases you have made. Is it consistently quoting prices or ranges of price that are realistic, based upon actual transactions in the marketplace? If not, the information provided is suspect.

### Guide Light

Richard Drucker, publisher of *The Guide* and of this book, gave me quite a chuckle some time ago. We were talking about the diamond section in his publication. I mentioned that I had been checking it against other sources, and had noticed that my last nine or ten diamond purchases (on memo) had been within two to three percent of the prices stated in *The Guide*. "Well," he responded, "I guess the dealers have finally figured out that I'm right, and they're pricing according to my figures!" This clever remark underscores the point. Price guides should report on the market ...not establish it! Not to be complacent, I continue to check diamond and colored stone purchases against *The Guide's* price grids and those of other publications.

Price lists are generally assumed to be accurate. After all, these are goods that someone is trying to sell. The stated asking prices have to be accurate, because we can hold the company to its word, right? Yes and no. I once had a difficult insurance replacement. None of my regular sources had what I needed, and there was some pressure to find a diamond quickly. I went to a publication that allows diamond dealers to list diamonds for sale, with many listings containing the information right off of the GIA or other laboratory's grading report. I made several calls to two different dealers, regarding particular listings they had published in this book. Even with my repeated efforts, and leaving specific messages regarding which diamonds

I wanted, neither called me back. The company I was with at the time had the highest Jewelers Board of Trade (JBT) rating possible, so I know that was not a consideration. After asking a few questions of other jewelers, I found out that certain dealers engage in "bait and switch" marketing in publications where they list goods. That is, they get the reader on the phone calling about a diamond that may not really exist. Then the caller will be presented with, "... that one was sold, but I have ...," and of course what is now available is more expensive. Lists can be deceiving, so know the source and verify its accuracy.

Ultimately, the estimate of value stated in the appraisal has to reflect reality in the retail marketplace. Up until now this chapter has dealt with wholesale sources. So we are back to the markup issue. It is one I do not like, because there is no absolute answer. The general answer might sound like double talk until you think it through. A simple example to follow would be that of a one carat diamond that would cost $3,500.00 to buy on memo, through a viable source in a major diamond center such as New York or Los Angeles. So what is it worth? What is a reasonable amount for which it should be insured?

That will depend upon your particular market area. In my local area, many if not most jewelers are happy with a 50% markup on such a diamond. Yet fifty miles away, where a jewelry exchange has established itself with the public as a solid source for diamonds, the markup on this diamond in some cases would be as low as 10%. The average seems to be about 20%. So jewelers within close proximity of that jewelry exchange have to take into account its effect on the marketplace, in terms of how jewelers react and what the resulting markups are. If traditional, independent jewelers in that area have lowered their typical

---

**Tell your customers: "The value is in the diamond, not in the paper."**

A jeweler/gemologist in the Northeast received a call from a long time customer, asking "What should a 3.69 carat pear shaped diamond, G color and VS$_1$ clarity, sell for?" The jeweler responded that it would depend upon factors other than just color and clarity. "Is $16,000.00 a good deal?" the customer asked. The jeweler's curiosity was aroused, and he asked the customer how she knew that the color and clarity were as represented. "I have the diamond in my possession, and it has a GIA certificate," was the response. "The jeweler who is selling the diamond encouraged me to call around to check out the price." In disbelief, the jeweler asked his customer to bring the diamond in so he could examine it.

The low price made sense once the diamond was revealed. It was "flat enough to fry eggs on," displaying little brilliance. "Simply put," the jeweler said, "it was ugly." The customers ended up buying a beautifully cut diamond of less than half the weight. But the story does not end there.

Several weeks later, a friend of the jeweler's, a gemologist/appraiser who had heard the story, received a call from one of *his* customers. "Is $16,000.00 a good deal for a 3.69 carat pear shaped diamond, G color and VS1 clarity?" Suppressing a chuckle, the appraiser asked, "Does it have a GIA lab report with it?" The customer responded that it did. "Does it look very shallow—flatter than it should?" was the next question. "Well, actually I was wondering about that," she replied. "How did you know?" "Did the jeweler tell you to call around to compare prices?" he asked. "Yes he did," she said, now becoming agitated. "How did you know *that*?" Unable to play the game any longer, the appraiser let the customer know that he had heard all about this same diamond just a few weeks before. Then he engaged her in a conversation about the importance of make in determining a diamond's beauty and desirability.

Appraisers have many opportunities to educate consumers. By doing so, we accomplish at least two important objectives. Not only do we elevate the public's perception of our industry, we may also be able to alert consumers to the differences between professional and not-so-professional jewelers.

markup on that diamond to 25% in order to compete more consistently, then it follows that the 25% markup is legitimate in estimating replacement cost for an insurance appraisal. The diamond is commonly available at that price, in that market area.

The point of this exercise is to illustrate how important it is to understand your market area for any product you intend to appraise. Markup surveys are regional, and may not reflect the conditions in your specific market area. So you have to be careful about blindly accepting statistics. They may not apply to the product you are appraising, in the area where you do business.

These assertions have been challenged by jewelers demanding, "How can I know what my competition is charging for a particular product? They will not give me that information. Why should they?" As usual the answer is not simple. But there are ways to get the information you need. As a jeweler you have many opportunities to discuss your customers' jewelry.

Depending upon the depth and familiarity of your relationships with your customers, some may happily volunteer information about what they paid for things they did not purchase from you. You can network with other jewelers through your state's Jewelers of America affiliate, and other industry organizations. If you are active in our industry, the information is available. You can also "shop" your competition. This is the dirty little word we do not like to use, but in reality jewelers are checking out each other's prices all the time. It is more likely that the "shopping" is for competitive reasons other than appraisal research, but it *is* a part of our industry. What better way to find out what things are selling for, than to put yourself in the position of a buyer?

So it is clear that standardized markup formulas will not work consistently. You have to know approximately how much the public is paying for a particular item in order to appraise it. The markup issue comes down to one thing: You have to know actual selling prices. A typical challenge to this assertion is, "Yes, but I have shopped my competition locally, and I know what their markup is on this particular item." If that is so, then you would also know how much the item sells for, and that is the connection that has to be made between markup and actual selling price.

### Designer and Artist Jewelry

There are two basic appraisal scenarios that occur with this kind of jewelry. In one case, you will have a signed, trademarked item that is easily traceable directly to the designer/manufacturer. By simply calling the manufacturing firm and describing or sending a photograph of the piece, you will be able to obtain a wholesale price. Even if you do not have a preexisting relationship with the maker, most are pleased when appraisers are professional enough to call, rather than guess the price. The markup issue comes up again, but manufacturers can often tell you approximately how much markup their retailer customers

> **What's it worth, anyway?**
>
> A Los Angeles jeweler was waiting on a customer, who asked to see a pair of silver earrings. As he removed the earrings from the showcase, the jeweler noticed that they bore the signature of Danish designer Georg Jensen. The earrings were 1940's vintage, and priced at $85.00. Realizing immediately what a bargain these earrings were at that price, the jeweler passed the information on to the customer, urging her to purchase them immediately. He informed her that if she did not, the pricing error would be corrected, and the earrings would be re-tagged at $350.00 The customer hesitated, then said she would like to think it over. Reminded once again that the price would be higher, she laughed and left the store. Three hours later, a different customer purchased the earrings—at the new price. Toward the end of the day the first customer came back to purchase the earrings. When told that the earrings had been sold, she stood still, eyes wide, dumbfounded. "You just don't want to sell them to me for $85.00," she accused. The jeweler responded, "I did tell you that the price would be corrected, and I did indeed sell them for $350.00." "Sorry," he said as he folded over the customer's name and displayed the invoice. She left the store once again ... only this time, she wasn't laughing!

are making on their products. If not, you will have to research that particular item. Generally, manufacturers or designers are very happy to provide you with the names of retailers in your area, who carry the line. Retail prices are then easy to find. If all fails (and this would be extremely rare), you might find out if the manufacturer would sell you one of these items in the event that a replacement were required in the future. If they would, you can make a note in the appraisal that your retail research was inconclusive, but the stated estimate of value reflects what *you* would charge to replace the item.

The other scenario is one in which you cannot actually contact the artist or designer directly. A good example would be an obscure artist in the Southwest. New Mexico in particular, is known for its Native American jewelry artisans. Some of them sell their work exclusively through galleries in Santa Fe or Albuquerque. This is yet another example of the value of the pre-appraisal interview. By finding out initially just where the piece was purchased, you will probably be able to contact that retail source directly to find out the correct, current retail cost. You may also obtain information about the artist, which may be valuable to your client or simply add-on material for your notes and future reference. In any event, galleries are generally happy to provide this information. A sharp business owner will understand that there is a benefit to providing you and your client (also their customer) with accurate price information. It encourages the client to return to them for replacement, should it become necessary.

## *Putting an item in its place*

Some time ago a jeweler on the East coast had a problem with a large department store chain. The department store had sent an employee out to obtain an appraisal on a ring the store was featuring in its jewelry department. Pretending to be a private party, the employee went to a local jeweler to have the appraisal done, allegedly for insurance purposes, and the jeweler of course complied. Later, the appraisal was found inside the department store's showcase, with the employee's name covered and replaced with, "To whom it may concern." The appraised value was several times the department store's selling price, making the appraisal a valuable selling tool when presented to customers as an independent opinion of value.

The jeweler/appraiser was outraged by this misuse of his work. He complained that, had he known what the appraisal was being used for, he would have appraised it based upon the kind of store it was selling in. Bingo! Except for one thing. The nature of the item should have been enough, and would have been enough for a professional, educated appraiser. The ring was a light weight, mass-production item, and typically sells in the kind of environment that this particular department store specializes in. The jeweler defended his appraisal by arguing that he had done his research properly. He had calculated the cost of duplicating the ring, assuming the making of a wax model, and casting and assembling a new ring. Unfortunately, this has nothing to do with how the ring would typically be replaced—at a department store, or through a discount jeweler who specializes in mass production jewelry.

## *How will the item be replaced?*

It is helpful in the appraisal process to ask this question about items being appraised. Where is this piece typically found? If you happened to be watching a home shopping channel last night and saw a blue topaz ring selling at fifty units per minute, for $99.00, then had a customer bring in that very ring, how would you assume it might be replaced? Through that home shopping channel, of course. If not there, then through a source that sells similar merchandise. You would not, in this obvious case, base your stated value upon the cost to make one such ring from scratch. In cases which might appear less obvious, it is advisable to use similar logic. In recent years it has become commonplace, and indeed a part of certain appraisal education standards, to include a statement about "expected manner of replacement" in the appraisal itself. This provides another bit of information that indicates you have done your homework and based your estimate of value on market reality.

### *Cost to reproduce: does it ever apply?*

The answer, of course, is yes. The cost of reproducing an item from scratch can be applicable, and the applicability of this methodology can be determined during the pre-appraisal interview. Make a habit of asking each appraisal client, "Is there any item among these that you would want duplicated identically in the event of a loss?" You will be surprised at the reaction. Most jewelry owners never consider this question until it is asked by an appraiser.

The following example will illustrate the point. A young woman insuring her jewelry brought 20 pieces to an appraiser. The appraiser asked the question and her reply was instantaneous. "Yes, this one," she said, pointing to a charm depicting a horse in its stall, with swinging gates on hinges. The charm would probably sell for around $500.00 as a production item. But this one was different. The woman's now deceased father had been a dentist. He had dabbled in jewelry making, and had specially designed and manufactured this charm for his horse-loving daughter. She made it clear to the appraiser, that whatever amount the charm had to be insured for, she absolutely would want it duplicated in the event of a loss. "It would not be the same one my dad made, but it would replicate it and always remind me of him."

The costs were calculated for recreating each component in wax, using the photographs and narrative description the appraisal would provide. Then the costs of casting, assembling, and finishing the piece were added, and the appropriate markup was applied, *for the appraiser's store*. A carefully worded addendum following the estimate of replacement cost explained the methodology employed, and also made clear that the stated amount reflected only that store's estimate to duplicate, and that the appraiser had not researched what other companies might charge. The appraisal and stated estimated retail replacement cost, based upon duplication, were accepted by the insurance company's underwriting department without question.

Of course if you do not do this kind of custom work in your store, you would want to research the cost of having such a job done, then explain your methodology in the body of the appraisal following the description and replacement cost estimate.

This scenario illustrates once again the importance of communication between appraiser and client. Any item you are not sure about should be questioned. When and how did your client acquire the item? Was it custom made? Was the process explained? What costs were involved at the time the piece was made? Is there any written documentation that might contain information useful to the appraiser? A client's response might be, "You're the appraiser. You tell me!" Make sure your client understands that his or her cooperation might provide the most direct, and therefore useful, research materials of all. The appraisal is for their protection, and they can help themselves by helping you.

This methodology will not work with all jewelry, however. Pieces that are signed by the artist and/or copyrighted designs have to be appraised differently. Ideally the artist or manufacturer should be contacted. This is the most direct, and therefore most accurate manner in which to obtain the information required to properly appraise the item. In fact, treating a copyrighted item as generic creates a very definite problem. Let us say an item is signed by an artist, and contains an international copyright symbol (©) and date along side the signature. If a design is truly copyright protected, you or any other jeweler would be in violation of that copyright when duplicating the item. This makes the cost-of-duplication methodology useless, as it implies the legitimacy of violating the copyright. A quote from the artist, or a gallery or other agent representing the artist, is the only truly accurate representation of replacement cost or value.

## Do not forget practical application

A reminder:  do not get so lost in all of the theory that you forget what we are trying to achieve with the insurance appraisal.  Before committing to an estimate of value (or replacement cost) in an appraisal, ask yourself the following question.  Can this item be replaced easily for that amount of money in my retail market area?  If the insurance company decided to cash out for the appraised amount, would the client have enough money to replace the item easily?  Would there be a significant amount of money left over?  The answers to these questions will help you to arrive at a reasonable dollar figure.

## Replacement cost vs. replacement value:  antics, semantics, or eccentrics?

Ultimately, the choice of either the word "cost" or "value" in your appraisals will be an individual one.  Traditionally, value has been used effectively because universally, people think they understand the word.  "What is this worth?" carries with it an expectation of a stated value as a reply.

It has become clear during appraisal sales presentations and pre-appraisal interviews, that the term **replacement cost** is more readily accepted and understood by the average client, than any term that employs the word "value."  Using "value" seems to automatically open the floodgates of misunderstanding, with terms like "market value" and "fair market value" slipping into the psyche of the client.  A term such as "estimated cost of replacement at retail," though unwieldy, is an option.

In an effort to be as clear as possible in communicating our appraisal, we should consider alternatives that might be more easily understood.  Back to basics.  When preparing the insurance appraisal, what are we trying to do?  We wish to convey a dollar figure of an amount that makes sense in terms of market reality, for replacement at the appropriate retail market level.  In essence, what will the item cost to replace?  In that sense of the term, *estimated retail replacement cost* seems to some appraisers to be more to the point, and less subject to interpretation.

Whatever your preference, be sure to define your terms in the appraisal.  There is no universal truth to impart regarding this terminology, except that it is important for anyone who relies on the appraisal to know what your terms mean in context.

## Closing thoughts

Remember your goal in producing an insurance appraisal.  It is easy to be distracted by the many issues that confront appraisers.  While the issues must be explored and dealt with, ultimately they do not have to be a distraction.  By taking into account all that you know at a given time, and applying the appropriate principles as a matter of habit, you will fall into a groove of sorts, and eventually find most insurance appraisals, and committing to specific values or replacement costs fairly straightforward.

Finally, keep your eyes on two prizes.  One is the immediate need to arrive at a reasonable, accurate assessment of an item's replacement cost.  The other is the larger prize, the attainment of a steady, profitable level of appraisal business that makes this arena interesting and worth pursuing.  The larger focus is a natural result of your becoming more comfortable with the dollar figures you commit to in writing.

R emember the jeweler from the previous chapter who was asked to appraise a light weight gold and gemstone ring? He was asked to appraise the ring for insurance purposes, and he complied in the best way he knew how. Unfortunately, the best way he knew how was not the best way. He believed that he had used the proper methodology by calculating the cost of reproducing the ring identically, then adding an appropriate markup to come up with a value of over $700.00.

As it happened, this jeweler was the victim of a scam of sorts. A major retailer had sent a "shopper" to the jeweler to have the ring appraised. The retailer then covered up the shopper's name and placed the appraisal in a store showcase with the ring—selling for less than half of the appraised value. The jeweler blamed the retailer, who had obviously behaved unethically by altering the document. But the jeweler set himself up for the proverbial kill by ignoring the fact that different market levels exist for jewelry. He treated a mass production item as though it had been a custom-designed item.

The cost for a jeweler to make one item is obviously and significantly higher than the per-item cost of making hundreds or thousands at a time. An item may appear in several markets, or nearly exclusively in only one. In any event, as appraisers we must be cognizant of the various retail markets available to the public.

Several years ago, appraiser/gemologist, James Coote began performing the mental exercise of listing as many retail markets as he could think of. These are markets, open and accessible to the general public, for jewelry of all kinds. Below you can see that list, with slight modifications. You will notice that the list contains outlets for new, used, antique, and period jewelry. As Mr. Coote stated with his original list, access to some of these markets requires aggressive, investigative shopping techniques. Others are easily accessed.

### *Retail Jewelry Markets Accessible to the Public*

*1.* Prestigious, status conferring jewelry firms. These are generally in major fashion centers and exclusive resort areas.

*2.* National or regional chain jewelry stores, located in shopping malls and larger shopping centers. Many use "acquired" old firm names.

*3.* Local chain jewelry stores, located in shopping malls, shopping centers, and/or downtown shopping areas.

*4.* Independently owned jewelry stores with a small number of units, located in shopping malls, shopping centers, or downtown shopping areas.

*5.* Independently owned jewelry stores, owner operated, located in shopping centers or downtown shopping areas. These are usually single units, stressing "owner in."

*6.* Upstairs jewelry stores, located in office buildings or industrial parks. These have a complete store appearance, and stress their low overhead and resulting lower prices.

*7.* National discount chain stores, emphasizing jewelry. Catalogs are available, and these stores present many special discount sales.

*8.*   Department stores, usually with a familiar local name and national ownership.  Leased jewelry departments are common, stressing often fictitious pricing such as "40% to 60% off."

*9.*   Specialty stores. These are fashion oriented, stressing accessories. Many have fine jewelry departments, some have leased departments.  These are less apt to manipulate prices.

*10.* Mail order catalog houses.  Expect mass produced, low to medium quality jewelry.

*11.* Boutiques.  These emphasize the trendy fashion image, many using designer makers, often on a consignment basis.

*12..* Seasonal boutiques, targeting Christmas.  Individuals or clubs rent space, usually selling consigned merchandise.

*13.* Antique shops, arcades and centers. These may be multi-dealer booth or single store entities.  Many show more period jewelry than actual antique pieces.

*14.* Antique shows, multi-dealer efforts, some with prestigious dealers.  These shows may be charity oriented, and some circuit-type shows are staged by promoters.  The shows usually take place in civic centers, auditoriums, and hotels.

*15.* Trade-Only gem and/or jewelry shows, large regional affairs, with care taken by sponsors to admit only qualified buyers, purchasing for inventory and eventual resale to the public.  Sometimes friends or relatives are brought in, and given access to the purchase of merchandise.

*16.* Publicly advertised gem and/or jewelry shows, staged by promoters, with admission granted to the public.  These are similar to the circuit shows mentioned in Item 14.

*17.*  Gem and mineral club shows, advertised and open to the public.  The jewelry making and gem cutting aspects are stressed, with some dealers selling tools, jewelry parts and findings, and some colored gemstones.

*18.* Door to door solicitation, mainly to homemakers with some samples to show and orders taken from catalogs, for later delivery.

*19.* Jewelry parties, presented by the host-seller, sometimes with the company representative present.  The host is rewarded depending upon sales volume.

*20.* Office solicitors, selling from jewelry trays and rolls.  These sellers go to easily accessible walk-in type offices, beauty salons, car dealerships, and small stores in shopping centers, such as beauty salons.

*21.* Trunk shows, in which dealers bring items in to dress shops, hair salons, and boutiques of all sorts, usually for one day at a time, only.

*22..* Car and street peddlers, who set up shop on a trunk lid, make quick sales, and are then gone.  Some set up a small table on a public street, which usually requires a city permit.

*23.* Pawn shops, selling out-of-pawn items and other new and used items.

*24.* Jewelry marts, from large multi-booth downtown locations to smaller scale operations in suburbs. Sometimes there are easily accessible offices near booth locations. Some go through depressed periods because of adverse publicity regarding underkarating of gold, money laundering scandals, misrepresentation of diamond quality, and abuse of so-called appraisals through overstatement of value by 50% to 200% or more. The "no sales tax if you pay cash" policy is very common in this marketplace.

*25.* Wholesalers to the public, easily accessible to consumers, usually in an office or showroom, often close to a major jewelry district.

*26.* Private dealers, who obtain consigned goods, often from marts or wholesalers. They sell to friends, neighbors, and relatives, strictly by word of mouth. They have little or no expertise, and rely on suppliers for grades, prices, and other representations.

*27.* Private individuals who wish to sell their own jewelry. Many use local newspaper classified ads as a marketing tool. They may also consign jewelry to their local jeweler, department store, or a major regional auction house.

*28.* Major international auction houses. Typically they charge 10% to 15% as a premium to both buyer and seller, based upon the hammer price. Some have a sliding scale according to the selling price. They have numerous sales each year, and the sales are well attended by both dealers and private buyers.

*29.* Major regional auction houses, with similar practices to international houses.

*30.* Court ordered or government agency ordered auction, usually for quick liquidation, i.e., "on the courthouse steps."

*31.* Itinerant auctions, usually set up on Sunday afternoons in hotels. These auctions often stress bronzes, oriental objects, and jewelry. Many employ pre-prepared appraisals with unconscionably high so-called insurance values.

*32.* Cable TV shopping channels.

*33.* Designer/artisan salons, offices, or boutiques.

*34.* Art shows and festivals. These take place in shopping center or school parking lots, downtown sidewalks, etc. They feature a variety of styles, from designer/artisan jewelry to mass produced items sold by the gram.

*35.* Flea markets and swap meets. These may feature closeouts, mass produced jewelry, collectibles, antique and period jewelry, items sold strictly by weight. Some say stolen jewelry is common in these venues .

*36.* Replacement companies who work with insurance companies. Some represent wholesale prices, and insurance companies do rely on them for legitimately discounted prices for satisfying loss claims.

*37.* Diamond dealers. Generally they are not accessible to the public, but some will help out friends, neighbors, or relatives.

*38.* Colored stone and pearl dealers. Same description as #37.

*39.* Jewelry manufacturers and true wholesalers. Same description as #37.

*40.* Trade shops and/or individual tradesmen (bench jewelers, setters, diamond cutters, engravers, watchmakers, etc.) who will obtain things for neighbors, friends, and relatives.

*41.* Jewelry supply houses, generally open to the public. They sell tools, supplies, jewelry findings, some finished jewelry, and sometimes colored gemstones and diamonds.

*42.* Independent appraisers, who may sell to selected clients. They may also broker items for clients, and usually do not maintain inventory. They generally work from catalogs and/or consigned goods provided by industry vendors. Note: Some define independent appraiser as someone who does not sell jewelry. For our purposes here, define the independent appraiser as someone who is appraisal-centered, independently of a retail operation.

*43.* Gem investment companies. These keep a low profile, and solicit almost exclusively by telephone, with a brochure or other literature as a follow up. "Buy from us and watch your investment grow" is a common theme. The problem surfaces, of course, when the investor decides to sell the gems. Who will buy them?

*44.* The Internet.

No doubt you have thought of some other markets in which the public can purchase jewelry. The exercise of listing and thinking about these markets is useful to appraisers for a variety of reasons. Knowing the vast resources available to jewelry buyers will open up your thinking when jewelry of a type you do not see every day comes to you for appraisal. Ask yourself, "Where is jewelry like this most often purchased?" The answer to that question alone might have helped the jeweler we discussed earlier avoid an embarrassing situation. He could have gone directly to the kind of retailer who carries such merchandise and conducted direct research.

The often-heard protest is, "I can't possibly go out to research every item that comes to me for appraisal." True enough. But appraisers are responsible for knowing the marketplace. That means ongoing research in a variety of markets, as well as that unique market that must be investigated from time to time for a special item.

By identifying markets and keeping them in mind as part of your research arsenal, you may be able to research many items directly in the market in which they are most often sold. Often your appraisal customer will be happy to share with you the origin of a particular item.

You may be asked to appraise items purchased at "60% off" from nationally known department stores. These are generally recent purchases, and the customer simply wants to feel better about a purchase that seems "too good to be true." In these cases, visit the department store if necessary, and price similar, if not exact, items at the source. To repeat, research does not get any more direct than this!

It is important in conducting research to be aware that it is actual transaction prices—not asking prices or tag prices—that are important to appraisers. For example, some department store fine jewelry departments routinely charge 50% of the tag price. Often, an additional 10% can be saved by opening a charge account at the time of purchase. When you are doing research in this kind of an environment, be sure to "shop" carefully. Find out what the public is actually paying for the piece.

The relationship between an item's most common marketplace and your value conclusion cannot be denied. You would not research a low grade promotional quality tennis bracelet on Rodeo Drive in Beverly Hills. Nor would you conduct a price study of a five carat ideal cut diamond at a pawn shop in a "low-rent district." If you had to appraise a ring that was similar or nearly identical to one that your neighbor bought from a television home shopping network, you would seek out that market to find out what similar rings sell for in that environment. (Then try to make sure your neighbor buys from *you* next time!)

So try a mental exercise of your own. Choose items that you see with some regularity as an appraiser. For example, try a diamond tennis bracelet, with diamonds set in a lower, commercial-quality 14 karat gold mounting. The diamonds are in the K through M color range, and $I_2$ in clarity. Where is such an item most commonly sold to the public? Examine the list provided, and decide where you would conduct price research if it was required.

Next try a traditional shell cameo set in a 1920's white gold frame. Where is such an item commonly sold? Play this game with various kinds of jewelry. If you continue this practice in your appraisal work, you will begin to find yourself attuned to the undeniable relationship between the proper marketplace for an item and that item's value.

## 7

*Nuts and Bolts*

## Anatomy of the
## Insurance Appraisal, Part I

Perhaps the key to insurance appraising can be summed up with the statement, "Do not assume your client or the insurance company know anything." This is not meant to be condescending or insulting to either party. But generally we cannot predict the level of expertise of any user of our appraisals, so we have to assume that everything relevant to securing proper insurance coverage should be included in the appraisal report.

This chapter will deal mostly with content, but will also touch upon cosmetics. Content is obviously of paramount importance because the appraisal is a communication device. However, your client's first impression of the finished appraisal product will be heavily influenced by its overall appearance.

A great deal of general information is assumed by most appraisers to be understood by the rest of the world. One example of this is our willingness to describe the metal in a piece of jewelry as "14 karat yellow gold." This seems fairly straightforward on the surface. But did you assay the piece? Are you certain that it is 14 karat gold throughout? Are you absolutely certain that assay would not determine it to be 13 karat? Admittedly, the odds of this ever becoming a problem are remote. But why take the chance when you can easily deal with any ambiguity that exists?

This chapter will explicitly spell out many of the issues that should be considered carefully as you develop your appraisal format. You may end up dismissing some as too esoteric or technical. Before you do so, consider again that as appraisers, we have to project the path our work will follow after it leaves our hands. So please please review all suggestions you find here.

### Cosmetics

Although this subject will be discussed further in Chapter 9, "Hyping the Typing: "Generating the Document," it bears mentioning here. An appraisal that looks professional will motivate your clients to read it. It is surprising how many of my clients over the years have called to compliment me on the content of my appraisals. Although I have often joked with clients that my appraisals are good reading material when they're having trouble getting to sleep, clients have often remarked that the appraisal "looked so professional" they could not resist the urge to read it word by word.

So cosmetics and content work together. We want the appraisal to be readable and contain all of the necessary information. We also want it to look professional and inviting, so that it will be read completely and we will gain the respect we deserve for the high quality of the content.

In the past the page or more that precedes the descriptive information in the appraisal has been called a ***cover page*** or ***cover letter***. Many appraisers have not been quite comfortable with this nomenclature, though many if not most have used the terms because appraisal societies prescribed them. There has also been some often humorous confusion about just what the cover letter covers. Because the CYA (cover your...well, you know, your assets) mentality has permeated appraisal courses, the "cover letter" has often been mistaken for something that covers the appraiser in terms of liability. Some simply accept the cover letter as similar to that which accompanies a job application and resume.

Actually, we are talking about an informational document-within-a-document, deserving of a term by which it can be identified. For the purposes of this discussion, I will coin the phrase ***Appraisal Information Document*** or ***AID***. Although the AID has its own name, it is a part of the appraisal and should be paginated as such. So if you have a three-page AID, eight pages of descriptive and value information, and a one-page professional profile summary, the appraisal is twelve pages long and the AID would be paginated, "Page 1 of 12, Page 2 of 12, and Page 3 of 12." This is an appropriate time to note that all appraisals should be paginated in the manner just noted. We are obligated to do this to assist anyone who might be presented with this appraisal at a later date. If an appraisal is presented to a third party and it begins with "Page 4 of 12," it will be obvious that pages are missing.

## THE APPRAISAL INFORMATION DOCUMENT: STRUCTURE AND CONTENT

This section is designed to guide readers in the creation of a boilerplate cover letter, one which can be used with all of your insurance appraisals—with minor modification to tailor it to the specific assignment.

As discussed in detail in Chapter 9, a computer, or at the very least some kind of word processor, is most helpful if not essential in generating professional appraisals. This section will make that abundantly clear, and computers will be mentioned to illustrate certain points.

The following suggestions are not all-inclusive. They are simply meant as a guide to generate the kind of thinking required to develop a complete AID. Some sample wording will be included. Readers must understand that the author's style and/or content are not necessarily appropriate for everyone. You should use this information as a guide, then develop your AID to suit your own appraisal style and methodology.

Once again, the need for formal appraisal education cannot be emphasized enough. This section is designed to alert readers to the issues involved. Only experience and education can fill in the blanks. And now to the "nuts and bolts."

### Why is the appraisal required?

The AID should state clearly why the appraisal is being performed, and what it may be used for. The terms *purpose* and *function* have been used to describe the "kind of value" and "what the appraisal will be used for," respectively. Without the words purpose and function defined in the appraisal itself, your client will not understand their specific meaning in the appraisal. Therefore, make sure that you define those terms within the wording of your AID.

Within the context of the AID, purpose states the type of replacement method being used to estimate the value of the item(s) being appraised. Estimation of retail replacement cost, fair

> ### Not all valuations are created equal
>
> An appraiser in California was asked by an elderly woman to appraise three items of fine jewelry. She wanted them appraised based upon their retail replacement values. She planned to use the appraisal as a guide in writing her will. She wanted to be sure that each of her three grandchildren received an equal value in property. The appraiser complied, and carefully explained the nature of the assignment and the meaning of "retail replacement value," in the Appraisal Information Document.
>
> One year later the appraiser received a call from an agitated young woman. Her grandmother (yes, the woman who had received the appraisal) had given her three pieces of jewelry to sell, in order to raise money toward the down payment on a house. She was angry because jewelers were consistently offering less than half of the retail values stated in the appraisal.
>
> "Have you read the first three pages of the appraisal, immediately before the description pages?" the appraiser asked. "Well, no I haven't," replied the young woman. "But I will." A few minutes later the phone rang again. "Now I get it," the woman said. "These values are retail. They have nothing to do with the amount someone would pay me for the jewelry!"
>
> Every appraisal—without exception—should clearly explain, the kind of value stated and the assigned use of the appraisal. Explain yourself before the fact, and you will have a much easier time explaining yourself *after* the fact.

market value, duplication cost, and forced liquidation value are all examples of purpose. Function states the ultimate use of the appraisal, such as obtaining or renewing insurance. Some appraisers have used the term ***intended use*** in place of function. While this is certainly clearer, ***assigned use*** is stronger, more concisely states that the appraisal may be used only as defined when the appraiser was retained, and is the term that we will use for our discussion.

It is also helpful to incorporate the number of items included in the appraisal into the first sentence of your AID. "This appraisal report, covering four (4) jewelry items, is prepared in order to estimate (or, if you prefer, "for the purpose of estimating") the retail replacement value(s) (or "cost of replacement" there is some debate over which term is more appropriate) of the items described herein, solely for the assigned use of obtaining or renewing insurance." This sentence makes clear at the outset, just why the appraisal has been prepared, and begins to inform anyone who relies on it that the appraisal may not be helpful if used for other purposes. Consider adding the following sentence: "Use of this appraisal report for resale or other non-insurance purposes is likely to mislead potential buyers or other third parties who may rely on the appraisal." This will alert anyone other than an insurance company that this appraisal is not intended for their use and that they should not rely on it, thereby limiting responsibility in the AID strictly to third parties that are insurance companies..

Let us imagine that Mrs. Smith has her used watch appraised by a local jeweler who has no formal appraisal education. His appraisals are not specific about how they are prepared or what their assigned use might be. He assigns a value of $3,000.00 to the watch. Several months later, Mrs. Smith decides to sell her watch and, coincidentally, someone she works with is interested. She innocently (or not) shows the appraisal to the prospective buyer, and as a result, this third party negotiates a purchase price of $2,000.00. What the unfortunate buyer doesn't know is that because this particular watch is still made and sells for $3000.00, the appraiser assumed that $3000.00 was the appropriate appraised value. In many cases this assumption is correct. However, in this instance the watch commonly sells in the secondhand marketplace for $1,500.00 or less.

By simply including the warning statement noted above, we might help the buyer to see that more research should be employed before making the purchase. This again illustrates the importance of paginating the appraisal. If Mrs. Smith decides to leave out the cover letter, a potential buyer or other inappropriate third party will still be aware that what has been presented is incomplete.


### *Basis of Value*

This section of the AID should make clear just what it implies. What is the basis for the value stated? Is it based upon replacement with a new item similar to the item being appraised? An example might be an appraisal of a six month old Rolex watch. Generally, insurance policies will replace such a used item with a new one. The same is usually true of a diamond engagement ring.

If the item a period piece, such as an Art Deco bracelet, it would be appropriately replaced with one of similar style and vintage. What if the item is a ring designed by your client's husband, then manufactured by a jeweler. It may be that nothing short of duplication of the ring would be satisfactory in the event of a loss. The following sentence is helpful in covering many of these possibilities: "Values stated reflect replacement costs for similar new items currently available or exact duplicates when indicated, except in the case of antique or period pieces or substantially, noticeably used pieces, in which case the stated value may be for replacement with a similar used item." This statement potentially covers a lot of territory, but begs certain questions. These questions must be dealt with somewhere in the appraisal. The most obvious is the issue of "exact duplication." Do not assume that an insurance company will automatically pay to reproduce an item.

If your clients want to have an item duplicated in the event of a loss, it is important that you make this very clear. It is recommended that you do so adjacent to the descriptive information, so that it is sure to be noticed by the underwriter—and, if a loss occurs, by the claims adjuster. For example, "Mr. and Mrs. Havegems have indicated that in the event of a loss, they would wish to have this item duplicated. Replacement with a similar item would not be acceptable. Therefore, the stated estimate of value is based upon **duplication** of the item."

This raises another issue...duplication by whom? If you base your estimate of value upon duplication in your store, say so. If you have contacted the jeweler who manufactured the piece originally and obtained a duplication quote from him or her, by all means include that information.

Other questions that might arise should be answered similarly, again, adjacent to the descriptive information so they will not be missed. The use of bold print and/or enclosing the statement in a box might also be helpful, and will demonstrate to your clients that you are looking out for their interests.

The value(s) stated in your appraisal also presumably have a basis in time. When are these values appropriate? Are they good for six months? One year? The fact is, we have no way of knowing if or when the replacement cost of an item might increase or decrease. We can know, however, what it costs today. So it is recommended that the appraisal and values contained in it apply only to a time you can research. Today. "The estimated value is based upon current information as of the date stated herein, and no representation is made regarding future value," is appropriate and clear.

There are some people who write appraisals who consider it a service to their clients to add an inflation factor to the appropriate current value of an appraised item. This is often as much as 20% to 30%. Needless to say (but let us say it anyway), inclusion of this factor does not serve your clients well. Even if inflation is a given (which it is not), the amount of a future price increase cannot be known today. Why subject your clients to additional insurance premiums for value they will never realize? They are better served by being advised to have their appraisal updated periodically.

You can generate insurance update business and bring your clients back into your store, by setting up a data base that reminds you to send out update notices. You can even refine your system to isolate specific items that are most likely to be subject to periodic increases. A dramatic increase in Rolex prices in 1995 illustrates that point.

Please see Chapter 11 for a detailed discussion of insurance replacements.

> As an aside it is interesting to note that price increases are not necessarily the result of manufacturers' desires to make a higher profit. When the value of the dollar drops significantly in relation to foreign currencies, certain products may increase in price automatically. The economy really *is* global!

## Sales tax

In the event of a loss, sales tax will be an addition to the basic cost of replacing an item. In most cases involving accurate appraisals, this is arguably not an issue. Let us say an item is properly appraised at $5,000.00. Continuing, we will say that when the loss occurs, the insurance company is able to successfully replace the item for $4,000.00. Even at 8%, which is high, the sales tax is only $320.00, for a total of $4,320.00. Although many insurance policies state that sales tax is not covered, in actual practice it usually is. If the total including sales tax does not exceed the coverage limit (appraised value), the tax will virtually always be paid by the insurer.

There are exceptions, however. During a very harsh winter in New Jersey, one insurance company was so busy with automobile and home damage claims that its claims adjusters were instructed to simply cash out claims such as jewelry losses. Using our same example, an insured who had to take a cash out settlement for the full $5,000.00, then make the replacement on his or her own at retail, might possibly have had to pay the sales tax, which with the 8% rate amounts to $400.00.

People buy scheduled jewelry coverage partly because they want 100% protection. Therefore sales tax is an issue that should be dealt with in the appraisal. For most appraisers, it is just as easy to include sales tax as not. This can be accomplished in two ways. One is to add the sales tax to each statement of value in the appraisal. You may find this unwieldy, and the solution is to simply include a total value for all items at the end of the appraisal (which you should do in any case), then a sales tax total, with a grand total to follow.

| | |
|---|---|
| Estimated retail replacement value, ten items: | $5,000.00 |
| 6% New Jersey sales tax: | 300.00 |
| TOTAL: | $5,300.00 |

If you choose not to include sales tax in your totals, that should be mentioned in your AID. Some stores operate at the borders of several states. Large chains, of course, generally operate in several states. A chain operating in several states and performing all appraisal services out of a centralized location, might choose not to bother with keeping track of the sales tax in every county of every state in which it has a store. I believe that this is a misguided decision because it does not serve the client.

Some relatively small geographical areas have varying sales tax rates. It is appropriate to base the sales tax rate upon where the client lives or frequently shops, making note of that fact in the appraisal or AID.

However, if you decide for any reason not to include sales tax, it is important that you inform your client. A simple statement in the AID can do the trick. "Sales tax: Due to the fact that Bigchain Jewelers operates in several states and appraisal services are centralized in our Seattle corporate offices, stated values do not include sales tax. We strongly recommend that our clients discuss with their insurance company the issue of sales tax as part of the cost of replacement." You have then alerted your client that sales tax is an issue, and given them the responsibility of pursuing the matter further. The sales tax issue in this scenario might lead you to ask about the variation in value from one store location to another. Value is a reflection of market activity, so like a specific sales tax rate, geographic location is always an issue.

### The role of the appraiser

This chapter began with the assertion that appraisers should assume that the insurance company and client know nothing about the appraisal process.

In fact, consumers are so much in the dark about what appraisers do (or are *supposed* to do!), that they commonly equate an offer to buy with an appraisal. Ask yourself— how many times have you been approached to do an appraisal, only to find that the customer actually wanted you to make an offer? In Chapter 16 dealing with ethics, we discussed the great care that must be taken to keep your "hats" hanging in separate places. Assuming that you do so, it is important to make it clear that you are not using your position as an appraiser to make a back door bargain purchase. Including the statement "This appraisal report is not an offer to buy or sell the appraised item(s) at any price" is a simple way to get that point across. Depending upon the nature of your business, and how involved your business (specifically your appraiser) is in over-the-counter purchases, you may choose to use stronger or more extensive language on this subject.

"The appraiser has no present, past, or contemplated future interest in the purchase, sale, or brokerage of the item(s) appraised." If this is not always true, you might preface the sentence with "Unless otherwise noted in the appraisal, ..." However you choose to word these statements, they should be designed to make clear the fact that you are maintaining an arm's-length attitude about the appraisal.

A statement about how fees are determined is also appropriate; if fees are per item, say so in this section of your AID. If you charge by the hour, state it. You need not state specifically what the charges are. The important point to emphasize is that there is no contingency fee arrangement. This means that you are not charging a percentage of the item's value (as stated by you). It also means that your fee for appraisal services is not dependent upon the client's success in purchasing insurance. What if your client has a credit problem and cannot find an insurer to underwrite the risk of their jewelry? You would still expect to be paid.

If you could somehow manipulate the facts (i.e., undervalue an item so it is less risky for the insurer, thereby making insurance easier to buy, with the promise that you will be paid if the client is successful), would you? We will presume not. You should make it clear that you are being paid to perform ethically and properly, and will not be influenced to manipulate values or other information in order to ensure that you are paid.

Do you generally examine, test, and otherwise gemologically inspect and document the jewelry you appraise? Or do you have a staff gemologist do that work, leaving just the valuation tasks for you? This section of your AID can provide that information. For example, "Unless otherwise stated, the property described in this appraisal was examined by the undersigned." is a good catch-all statement to include if you almost always do all of the inspection of the jewelry yourself. On those occasions when you might rely on someone else's labor, you can add a note in the description portion of the appraisal, or simply change the AID wording for that one appraisal. If you regularly rely on others' labor, you of course would use the appropriate wording to say so.

## Documentation

Although you might tire of hearing this, assume once again that your clients know nothing about the appraisal process. We should also assume that they are not experts in photography (nor are most appraisers!). Regardless of what kind of photography you choose for your appraisals, it is important that users of the appraisal do not assume colors are accurate enough to use to duplicate the original color of an item if there is a loss. "Photographs included in this appraisal report are for the purpose of design representation and documentation only, and should not be relied upon for accurate color reproduction, clarity, brilliance, or size." Follow this statement by a sentence or two about how these qualities *are* recorded and described, to explain this concept in an easily understandable manner.

You might also answer a question that is commonly asked, before it is asked, by stating that you retain copies of every appraisal in your files. If the time period for which you retain these files is limited, say so. State also that these files are confidential, and that they will not be shown or released to anyone other than your client unless you are legally compelled to do so. This might seem like overkill, but these issues are asked about frequently, and it will provide additional peace of mind if you state your policy in writing.

In a contract for services that I used for several years, I included a statement promising confidentiality. I was once contacted by the estranged spouse of a former appraisal client of mine, demanding to see copies of appraisals I had done for her husband. I explained that the appraisals were confidential, and that I could not release them without her husband's written consent. Exasperated, she snorted, "If I could get my husband to release them, I wouldn't be calling you!" I said that I understood, but that I had made a written promise of confidentiality to her husband. "Well if you won't provide those copies to me, I'll have my lawyer get the court to subpoena the appraisals, and then you won't have any choice but to release them." "Ma'am," I replied, if you have the appraisals subpoenaed, I will release them gladly. My agreement states that I will not release them unless I am 'legally compelled' to do so. I have no intention of going to jail to protect your husband's confidentiality. That subpoena would compel me, wouldn't it?" "Oh," was her response. Upon hearing of the impending scenario, the husband released the copies voluntarily. In any event, it is important for our clients to know that we value their privacy. This discussion leads us to ownership of our files. It is recommended that an attorney be consulted in this regard, perhaps to establish the appraiser's ownership contractually. Otherwise beware: your files may not belong to you if possession is challenged.

### *Identification and quantification of materials*

In the introductory part of this chapter, an example of 13 karat gold, marked "14 karat" was used. Once again, it is important to remember that our clients make certain assumptions. One is that if you say in your appraisal that a ring is "14 karat yellow gold," it is indeed 14 karat. Not 12.5, or 13 karat...14 karat. This is, of course, unless you clarify the limitations on your ability or willingness to test each piece. Even if you do test each item, how accurate you can or cannot be should be noted. It is also acceptable to simply state, "stamped '14K'," if you include a statement in your AID that establishes clearly that you rely upon the quality stampings on the items.

You have no doubt encountered, or will encounter, a ring with an 18 karat gold top and a 14 karat shank. Maybe you have seen a ring with a platinum top, 14 karat white gold shank, entirely plated in yellow gold. Even touchstone ("acid/scratch") or electronic testing have limits. Unless you melt your customer's piece into a ball, then have it assayed professionally, you will never be certain of the purity or uniformity of the metal quality in an item you appraise. Even if such extreme destructive measures were taken, you would obtain only an average karat purity, rather than specific information. I dare to say that your appraisal business would not last long if you began melting clients' jewelry (specific gravity and other tests are available to jewelers to help prevent such extreme measures).

But how do you convey information to your clients about the quality of materials without rewriting this entire book, and just as importantly, without diluting their confidence in your ability? Sit back for a moment and think about how extensively you test the metal composition of appraised items. Then explain. Assume for a moment that you generally rely upon the quality stamped on metals. Perhaps you test one area to achieve reasonable assurance that the "14K" piece is not silver or brass. And when you do test, how accurate are your methods? Now study this statement. "Metal quality (i.e., 14K gold) is assumed to be consistent throughout a particular item, with that of the specific area tested and/or of the quality stamped or otherwise marked on the item, unless otherwise stated in the appraisal. When testing is deemed necessary, it is by the touchstone ("acid/scratch method"), which is generally accurate within 1 to 1.5 or 2 karat."

Gemstone weights and measurements are also of concern to our clients. Consumers assume that we have ways of knowing things. They have a right to assume so, unless we explain otherwise. Unless you remove and weigh gemstones, the weights you state are estimates. How do you compute these estimates? Are they based upon formulas? Are these formulas of your own creation, or are they promulgated by an educational organization (GIA perhaps?) and commonly used and accepted by appraisers and gemologists? These questions can be answered in a sentence or two, and should be.

## *Diamond grading:  subjective objectivity*

We have learned through the trade press, and even from the Gemological Institute of America itself, that there are few if any absolutes in diamond grading.  It is important that our AID convey that fact without destroying consumer confidence.  What are the facts?

*a.* Two trained graders might disagree on a color or clarity grade.

*b.* Lighting conditions, time of day if outside light is present, and fatigue can all affect the ability to color grade effectively and consistently.

*c.* Color comparison sets are only as good as a human being's ability to grade them accurately.  (Some Cubic Zirconia sets have been known to exhibit color shift under certain conditions.)

*d.* Diamonds that are mounted are more difficult to grade, particularly for color.

Does all of this mean that we cannot grade diamonds and state our opinions in an appraisal? Of course not.  What it *does* mean is that we have to illustrate the limitations to our clients. Some appraisers resort to splitting grades, stating for example "H-I" or even "H-I-J" color. Many gemologists have been taught that the three-grade range is not only acceptable, but preferable for mounted diamonds.  But in the event of a loss, this method will leave both your client and a flustered claims adjuster wondering which of the grades to apply to the claim and eventual replacement.  Therefore, except in extraordinary cases, it is preferable to commit to a grade, with your AID explaining clearly what the limitations are.  The above four facts can be included as you deem appropriate to your equipment and the conditions under which you grade diamonds.  I also suggest the following, in addition to the other stated limitations.  "Due to the limitations  created by the mounting, diamond color and clarity grades should be considered provisional, and might be changed by the undersigned if graded out of the mounting at a later date."

It is acceptable to declare a split color grade, as long as the one used to determine your estimate of value is clearly noted.  Some appraisers consistently give the diamond the benefit of the doubt, and will clearly state that this is the case whenever a split grade is used.  One appraiser uses both master comparison diamonds and an electronic diamond grading instrument. He might state, "Master comparison diamonds resulted in a color conclusion of 'G', and the Brand X color grading instrument indicated 'H.'  'G' was used for valuation purposes."

Some appraisers will not assign a Flawless, Internally Flawless, or even VVS$_1$ clarity grade to a mounted diamond.  Some are reluctant to assign a color grade of "D" or possibly "E." This can be decided on a case by case basis.  Obviously a one carat diamond set in a tall white gold setting with thin prongs is easier to grade than the same sized diamond in a yellow gold bezel.  Whatever your decision, it should be explained in either your AID or in the description portion of the appraisal.  For example, if you suspect a diamond may be "D" color but are unwilling to assign that grade (even provisionally) while it is mounted, you might suggest verbally to your client that the diamond should be removed for more accurate grading.  If your client is not willing to have this done, say so in the appraisal.  This covers you in the future if the client forgets your discussion, and informs the insurance company that there is some doubt. The rest is up to those two parties unless you are later asked to go further.

*Caution!!* If you do have permission to remove a diamond for weighing and/or grading, be sure that this is done in a very controlled environment.  That means your client has the opportunity to watch you remove the diamond in his or her presence, grade and weigh it to your satisfaction, then positively identify it with either a plot diagram or photomicrograph, and a good look by your client through the microscope.  Point out any outstanding characteristics, in addition to plotting or photographing them.  Ideally, the diamond should be reset in the presence of your customer as well.  The more care you exercise, the more remote the chance that you will be accused of switching or damaging a diamond. Remember, the accusation can come from the original selling jeweler. So even assuming a trusting relationship between you and your client, it is advisable to have a statement prepared, acknowledging the care that was taken and procedures followed, to be signed by your client for your protection.

### What about diamonds accompanied by lab reports?

Frequently you will be asked to appraise an item containing a diamond that is accompanied by a laboratory diamond grading report. These reports are prepared by human beings and as such are subject to the same kinds of subjectivity we have already discussed. However, and of course depending upon the particular laboratory, the grading may be more consistent than that of the average gemologist working in the retail environment. This is because laboratory graders see and grade many more diamonds than most of us do, and generally under very controlled conditions. Additionally, some labs state that three graders are involved in every report. When this is the case, it would also contribute to greater consistency. But let us not forget that, even if three out of five graders agree on one grade, the two who dissent may be correct! "Scientific subjectivity" is the order of the day in diamond grading.

There is no rule, written or unwritten, that states we must defer to a lab report's findings. You may disagree strongly with a lab report, and if you do and are confident of your own ability and the conditions under which you work (lighting, master comparison stones, etc.), use your grade(s). However, some explanation will have to be provided as to why this laboratory report is being set aside in favor of your opinion. Your client is likely to believe that this laminated, formal lab report is more valid.

Arguably, the Gemological Institute of America/Gem Trade Laboratory (GIA/GTL) report is considered the most valid source for most of our industry. To a degree, that belief may be justified. After all, GIA did invent the diamond grading nomenclature that is most widely used in the diamond and retail jewelry industries. Because of sound marketing and generally very consistent grading standards, GIA/GTL has established itself (whether intentionally or not) as the last word in diamond grading. "Let's send it to GIA" is the clarion call of many a jeweler trying to smooth ruffled feathers or settle a dispute over a grade.

Other laboratories have established varying degrees of credibility in the industry. In any event, how you use those reports should be explained somewhere in your appraisal. If you wish to defer to reports issued by certain laboratories, say so in your AID. For example, "If a diamond is accompanied by a laboratory report prepared by the GIA/GTL, Fred's Diamond Grading, Inc., Diamonds R Us, or the Diamond Lab of Mozambique, and the diamond can be verified as being that diamond described in the report, the undersigned appraiser may defer to the laboratory's assessment." Just be sure to note in the appraisal itself that the diamond is accompanied by such a report, and that you have matched the diamond to it and chosen to defer to the laboratory's opinion.

If you disagree with a laboratory report, state that the report exists, describe it by laboratory, number, and date, and state that you have graded it differently. You might disagree and state the difference, while still basing your value conclusion upon the lab's grade. Just be sure to make this clear in the appraisal. Whether or not an insurance company accepts your grading is another issue. I doubt many underwriters have encountered appraisers with the nerve to disagree with a lab report in writing—and this is not a recommendation that you do so, or not. It is simply meant to keep us all on our toes. Diamond grading is a subjective science, and qualified graders sometimes disagree. An underwriter certainly has the option of contacting you for further reinforcement of your opinion, as long as he or she knows what your opinion is.

## Condition

An item's condition is of great importance to both the insured and the insurance company. Frequently a consumer will suddenly notice a chip or other damage on a diamond or piece of jewelry, which they had not noticed previously. This may be because the damage is new, or simply because they happened to be sitting under a bright light contemplating the item for some reason. By noting condition of items you appraise, you can alleviate doubts that arise on the part of both consumers and insurance companies about whether a damage loss is insured or not.

### Something to Watch Out For

People in general do not know their possessions as well as they think. One jeweler has a unique way of dealing with the kind of customer who states "that scratch wasn't there before" when, for example, retrieving a watch after a battery change. First the jeweler explains the process of changing the battery, including the fact that it is placed crystal-down on a soft pad, etc., and that there is no way the dial, for example, can be scratched in the process. Often the customer insists, "I know that watch. I wear it every day, and I know that scratch wasn't there." Next, the jeweler asks the customer to hand him the watch. He then proceeds to ask very specific questions about the watch's dial. What style are the numbers? Are they Arabic or Roman numerals? Are they painted, enameled, or applied? What color are they? What does the second hand look like? What color is the dial? In almost every case, the customer cannot answer even these simple questions. The jeweler then gently explains that if these original features of the watch have not been noticed sufficiently to remember them, how can the customer insist that a scratch would have been noticed? This usually gets the point across, and illustrates that we have to write an appraisal that will serve as our client's memory in the event a question arises about condition or other qualities or characteristics of their jewelry.

The issue of condition can be dealt with in a fairly simple way. Try dividing condition descriptions into three categories. *"New,"* can describe an item that you know to be brand new, or one that shows a minute amount or no sign of wear or deterioration. *"Normal wear"* denotes an item which may contain scuffing, light scratches, or other wear that would occur in the normal use of an item of the approximate age of the item in question. Such an item probably would appear "like new" with light polishing and cleaning. *"Other characteristics"* can be described independently of the specific designations you decide upon. You will develop terminology that suits your own preferences, but these guidelines give you the idea. One appraiser likes the term "pristine" to describe a used item that is in new condition. The important point is that condition should not be ignored. To do so is unfair to an insurance company that will rely on your appraisal. Damage not noted in the appraisal may be noticed later by the insured, resulting in an erroneous insurance claim, and either bad feelings toward an insurer that refuses to pay, or an unfair burden of payment on a more cooperative insurance company.

# 8

*Soup to Nuts*

# Anatomy of the
# Insurance Appraisal, Part II

## *Gemological Information: Useful, or wasteful?*

There has long been debate about how much related gemological information should be added to the appraisal for the client's benefit. Many if not most jewelers involved in appraising consider such information non-essential, or even a ridiculous waste of time and paper. "Insurance companies do not care about all that fluff," they say. If you are one who agrees, perhaps this section will open your eyes and get you to think differently on the subject. There are elements that insurance companies may indeed "not care" about, but those elements may still prove helpful to your client when he or she tries to understand and deal with an insured loss.

One appraiser I know includes two pages about gemstone enhancements at the back of every appraisal report. This is the complete list generated by the American Gem Trade Association and others several years ago. This appraiser finds the inclusion of the entire list preferable to focusing on the client's particular gem or gems, because it informs the client of the possibility of treatment, without causing a panic by pointing out that "virtually all emeralds are treated in some fashion," for example. Of course any specific treatment noted during the examination should be described, but including the information pages covers the possibility of undetected treatments.

A good example would be that of ordinary, commercial quality blue sapphire. Most blue sapphire is heat treated for one reason or another, but because this treatment is considered usual for this stone and is generally not easy to detect, its disclosure is generally ignored. By including the gemstone enhancement information as an addendum, you have at least given your client the opportunity to read about enhancements that are sometimes or often present in sapphires and other gemstones.

Diamond grading nomenclature, though part of the common language of most jewelers, is professional jargon to the average consumer. So it is very helpful to add a page explaining the GIA (or other, if it is appropriate and you use it) nomenclature. This can be pre-printed as an addendum to your appraisal, so that you do not have to print out the page every time you print an appraisal. But find a way to add this information to your appraisal when diamonds are involved. Though initially it may appear to you to be "fluff," your clients will often read the entire page, and may even thank you for being so thorough and conscientious.

Once again, assume that your clients and their insurance companies know nothing about jewelry. They probably cannot define "cultured pearl." Yet that is a term we regularly use in our appraisal descriptions. So in addition to the other information we have discussed here, a glossary is recommended. This can usually be accomplished, once again, with one addendum page. Before dismissing this idea as yet another burden that wastes paper and nobody cares about (you see, I *did* read your mind), consider the following list of commonly used terms and abbreviations. Think about how many, or should I say how few of these, your clients understand or can define.

| | |
|---|---|
| "ct." for carat | cultured pearl |
| "dwt." for pennyweight | fluorescence |
| gold-filled | gold plated |
| "gm." for gram | inclusion |
| "KT." for karat | mabe pearl |
| modern brilliant cut | old European cut |

| | |
|---|---|
| old mine cut | 90/10% platinum/iridium |
| rolled gold plate | saturation |
| single cut | sterling silver |
| synthetic | tone |
| white gold | yellow gold |

Although most of the terms are commonly heard and some even used by your clients, few are really understood. By adding a pre-printed glossary as an addendum to your appraisal, once again you will have shown how conscientious you are, and how important it is to you to educate and inform your clients.

## DESCRIBING GEMSTONES

### *Diamonds: How much information is enough?*

This is one of the many questions in appraising that has no specific, clear-cut answer. Part of the process of becoming a professional appraiser involves gaining the insight required to make judgments about your own format, style, and content requirements. Certain basic criteria should be considered regarding diamonds.

The size and quality of the diamond will have some bearing upon how much detail you include in your description. It would serve no practical purpose to analyze crown angles and table percentages on the fifty, five-point diamonds in a cluster ring. A general description including the range of color and clarity (i.e., G to H color, SI clarity, good polish, fair to good symmetry) is usually sufficient in this case. Some appraisers prefer to use "colorless," "near colorless," and so on, and this is acceptable as long as those ranges are defined in the appraisal.

A 1/4 carat diamond solitaire engagement ring requires more information. The diamond is the central component of the ring, and will be the focus of any replacement scenario that might develop in the future. In this case, more detail about the diamond's cutting proportions is appropriate and necessary. For example, you might decide upon dimensions, estimated weight, color, clarity, overall depth percentage, and a plot diagram to adequately describe this diamond.

Does the amount of detail increase as the size of the diamond increases? Possibly. It is helpful to develop a minimum standard for yourself. For example, "I will include all of the above for any engagement ring diamond over 1/4 carat in weight. For diamonds over 1/2 carat I will do a more complete analysis, adding crown angle, pavilion depth percentage, table percentage, culet size, girdle thickness, and any other proportion and cut characteristics I am able to measure or estimate, and document." This is arbitrary, of course, and it is generally preferable to use these decisions only as guidelines. Be sensitive to the needs (both emotional and practical) of your clients as individuals.

Other factors that have to be considered are inclusions that may negatively impact on the durability of the diamond; proportion or shape irregularities in fancy shapes; "bow ties" visible in marquise, pear shaped and oval diamonds; flat lobes or shoulders; strong fluorescence; and other characteristics that influence value in the marketplace. Again, every appraisal has its own implications and nuances, and it is the job of the appraiser to determine when, how, and what to include in the appraisal. Even those items you may choose to omit might be helpful at a future time, if recorded in your notes.

Table percentage presents a clear example of the influence a particular characteristic can have on value, and ultimately on an insurance claim. Imagine that you are a replacement vendor, and receive a quote request for a round brilliant cut diamond that is defined in the accompanying appraisal simply by its weight, color, and clarity. Based upon that information you know that the diamond normally retails for around $4,000.00 in your area, based upon a wholesale cost of $2,800.00 for diamonds of better make.

You are informed that the policy holder has $3,100.00 of insurance coverage, and the policy was underwritten based upon a recent appraisal. You will have to assume that the diamond is underinsured that the stated value is too low. Aha, but here's the surprise. I forgot to build into the scenario the fact that the lost diamond had a 71% table. Of course it is gone now, and nobody will ever know that the $3,100.00 stated value was probably very accurate. Had the appraiser included that noteworthy information in the appraisal, your job as the replacement vendor would have been simplified.

Perhaps the competitive spirit in you is saying, "Why should I make things easier for another jeweler?" The answer is simple. The jeweler who is replacing the diamond under these circumstances, having been apprised of the 71% table, would be in a position to discuss replacement options with the insured. Perhaps they would like to have a diamond cut to better proportions, and would be willing to give up weight, color, or clarity in order to do so, or add additional money for better make. By including all pertinent information, you make a claim that may have to be dealt with in the future that much easier for your customer to endure.

So whatever decisions you make about item descriptions, always keep in mind the needs of your client. If this diamond is lost, what information will be required to replace it with a diamond that is truly of like kind and quality? That question should be the basis of not only this decision, but of your thinking in general regarding appraising for insurance.

## Asked, answered...ignored

An East Coast appraiser was hired to write an insurance appraisal for a diamond engagement ring. He was apprised of the GIA/GTL diamond grading report that had been supplied when the diamond was purchased two years prior. Asked by the client if he would like to see the lab report, the appraiser declined. He graded the diamond I/VS$_1$ and appraised it accordingly. There was one slight problem, however. The GIA/GTL report, which he never availed himself of, stated **G** color and **VS$_2$** clarity. This upset the owners of the diamond, who returned to the selling jeweler to protest his alleged misrepresentation. Fortunately, sanity prevailed. The jeweler and the professional appraiser he had on staff were able to demonstrate the folly of the first appraiser's methodology. Any documentation that is available to the appraiser should at least be inspected. You can always reject or disagree with a document, but it cannot help you if you ignore it. It is an advisable practice to ask your appraisal clients, "Do you have any previous documentation for any of these items?" You never know what you might find...perhaps even a GIA/GTL diamond grading report!

## To plot, or not to plot?

In response to an article published in *National Jeweler* in 1994, a letter to the editor exclaimed, "Plot diamonds? Ralph, you must be kidding!" The letter went on to assert that to expect plot diagrams, except in extreme cases, was asking too much of appraisers. One appraiser once commented that appraising is "not brain surgery," and "diamonds are rarely if ever recovered by police after a theft," therefore plotting was not important.

Plotting diamonds is not an absolute. As with much of what has been written and taught about appraising, you must make decisions about how much of that information you assimilate into your appraisal procedures. But take care to make those decisions based upon your increasing knowledge, rather than upon your need for convenience. The decision about whether or not to plot diamonds will be based upon several factors.

Some appraisers draw a seemingly arbitrary line. One guide I read stated absolutely that any diamond over 1/4 carat should be plotted in the appraisal. Others plot 1/2 carat and larger diamonds, some begin at 3/4 carat or a full carat, and no doubt there are appraisers who plot only when the urge strikes them. One particular appraiser plots every diamond weighing over 1/4 carat. A tennis bracelet containing forty 1/4 carat diamonds will be documented with forty plots, all numbered according to placement in the bracelet. Expensive? Yes. Necessary? Well, no. But the answer was a resounding, "Yes," according to that appraiser! His rationale? By listing the diamonds in order and plotting each one, any diamond out of that bracelet that had to be replaced in the future would be replaced more accurately. Realistically though, tennis bracelets are almost always manufactured with consistent diamond quality throughout. This makes plotting all of the diamonds would seem to be overkill.

We have all been tempted at one time or another to omit what we know to be an important step in the documentation process, possibly because of time constraints or even just plain laziness. Obviously we cannot follow these inclinations when it comes to our clients' welfare. The key here is balance. You should develop your own criteria for making the "to plot, or not to plot" determination, then be as consistent as you can.

The following is a true story. A woman was watching television, absent-mindedly running her finger over the girdle of her mounted, one carat engagement diamond. She felt a "chip" that she had not noticed before. The diamond had been appraised by the seller two years previously, then appraised by another jeweler a year later when she changed insurance companies. Neither appraisal contained a note regarding anything irregular or unusual. In fact, upon examining the two documents it became clear that they had not made note of much at all.

Inspection of the diamond revealed a fracture emanating from the girdle, extending to the opposite side of the table. We would all agree that this is a significant clarity characteristic. The seller's appraisal was so inaccurate as to color grade (off by four to five grades) that their assessment of $VS_2$ clarity could not necessarily be relied upon either. The later appraisal was also off by several color grades, so the stated clarity grade of $SI_1$ would have to be considered suspect as well. Neither document contained a plot diagram or any description of the grade-setting inclusion or inclusions.

The woman had just filed a claim with her insurance company. Asked to inspect the ring and determine whether or not the fracture was damage, I was put on the spot. None of the documentation seemed reliable. Anyone who could grade color so inaccurately and provide so little information in the appraisal could probably not be relied upon to have seen the fracture. I told the insurance company and the policy holder that I could not say with certainty whether the fracture was new. Eventually the claim was settled with cash, but only after much grief and wasted time experienced by the policy holder. If you ever find yourself in this situation, the GIA Gem Trade Laboratory does issue damage reports. But always be aware of how you, as an appraiser, can help to abbreviate the claims process by providing complete, accurate documentation.

The case described makes a strong argument for plotting diamonds. Had either of the appraisers included a plot diagram or verbal description of inclusions without any documentation of such a prominent inclusion as that fracture, the insurer would have been much more likely to assume that the fracture was new. After all, someone who was careful enough to diagram or describe inclusions would most likely have been careful enough to see something so obvious. This sentiment was also expressed by the adjuster who handled the claim.

Another reason to plot? It looks professional. One jeweler once said, "I think we should plot even when it's not really necessary—because it looks so cool." A surprising number of customers will ask for "one of those plot things," when they submit a diamond for appraisal. Many who do not specifically request a plot will always want one in the future after it is provided for the first time. So for promotional purposes alone, plotting is worth considering. And although the odds are against it, diamonds are occasionally switched by dishonest jewelers. Imagine what a hero you would be if your plot diagram proved conclusively that the customer's diamond had been switched. It might also save an innocent jeweler by proving the diamond was *not* switched.

### Hit Her With a Switch

A highly trusted and respected independent appraiser was asked to appraise a diamond ring for a customer of a local retailer. The steamer and ultrasonic cleaner were located out of the customer's view. The ring had not been sufficiently cleaned for proper examination, so the appraiser excused himself and went to the back room to clean the ring properly. Having done so, he returned three minutes later.

Several weeks later the customer decided that, during those three minutes, the appraiser had switched her diamond. Considering that the old, worn prongs were still perfectly in place, this of course was unlikely. The woman filed a lawsuit. The story gets very interesting.

During the miscellaneous legal processes, the woman somehow determined that the diamond in fact had not been removed from the ring. She accused the appraiser of having a selection of similar rings in the back for the deliberate purpose of making such substitutions. So now her accusation was that the entire ring had been swapped.

Several years prior to this incident, this woman had remounted her diamond through this same store. The allegedly substituted ring bore the trademark of the remount company that had provided the original ring. This helped to convince the court that no switch had taken place. To this day, however, the customer still believes that the appraiser switched the diamond.

But the story does not end here. Prior to the unsuccessful lawsuit, the woman had the ring appraised by nine other appraisers. Because there was not general agreement with our original appraiser, the woman said that she had positive proof that he had switched the diamond. His color grade was higher than any of the other nine appraisers who grade the diamond. His clarity grade was higher than most, lower than none. This, said the woman, was positive proof that he had switched the diamond. Everyone was reporting lower quality than he did!

Several of the appraisers were interviewed during the deposition process prior to the trial. They were asked about their diamond grading techniques, and in particular what kind of comparison stones (if any) they had employed. The jeweler whose appraisal had been given the most weight by the woman, testified that he had color graded the diamond by comparing it to his shirt sleeve.

Rumor has it that the GIA's Gem Instruments store is now selling shirt sleeves.

So what is the answer? Every appraisal assignment must be considered individually. The needs or expectations of the client, along with the nature of the jewelry and the assigned use of the appraisal, must all be considered.

In the case of the tennis bracelet with forty, 1/4 carat diamonds, plotting does not serve a practical purpose. In almost all cases, tennis bracelets are set with a narrow and consistent range of diamond qualities. To describe the bracelet as containing forty diamonds, with clarity noted as "SI" or "SI$_1$ through SI$_2$," for example, is acceptable. If all but five are the higher (or lower) of the two grades, say so. But except under extraordinary circumstances (for example, the client requests it, or litigation is involved), it would seem to be overkill. In a replacement scenario involving one or several diamonds, or the entire bracelet, the plots would have little if any impact on the handling of the claim.

But now let us look at a single 1/4 carat diamond, the only diamond in your client's engagement ring. In this instance, a diamond of this size takes on a different significance. Your newly developing criteria might dictate that you plot this diamond, or describe the grade-setting inclusion(s).

As a rule of thumb (since by now you're probably looking for one), plot the main or center diamond in any engagement ring. This is an important piece to your client, and often the only item she will separately insure with a policy rider.

A brooch, pendant, or bracelet might also contain a primary diamond. Depending upon the size and quality of such diamonds, you should also consider plotting them. And of course you have to consider the possibility that you will someday have to appraise a tennis bracelet with 1/2 carat diamonds. Is a plot of each and every diamond justified or necessary? On a case by case basis, you will have to make that decision. Often it will depend upon the desires of your client. If she wants every diamond plotted, you certainly have an opportunity to charge a much higher fee. But ask yourself how important this is, and what percentage of your customers will pay for this service, as opposed to the number who might think you are looking for ways in which to pad your fee.

The comment is often made, "I cannot possibly charge enough to justify the time it takes to plot diamonds." This is a valid concern, but if you include plotting in your repertoire, you might be surprised. You might offer plotting as an extra, and charge a set fee for each plot provided.

One particular appraiser never plots unless it is requested. He is very careful, however, to address the absence of plots in his appraisals. Your AID and Contract For Services can include a statement similar to the following: "Plot diagrams are not included with the appraisal unless requested by the client. It should be noted that the absence of a plot might make identification of the diamond more difficult in the event of loss, damage, or other scenario requiring proof of the diamond's specific internal characteristics." This statement informs both the client and insurance company that the issue was considered, and what the ramifications are of the choice not to include the plot diagram.

This discussion about plotting may be frustrating for some readers. We naturally expect a book to provide concrete answers. Although this book is intended to provide many, appraising is not an absolute science. Many issues in appraising have to be discussed—we cannot ignore them. Yet there is room for flexibility, and the decision-making process is enhanced by experience, education, and careful study of your clients' needs on a case by case basis.

A final note on plotting: Technology seems to be gradually replacing plotting as a means to record diamond characteristics. Both video and still imaging technologies are infinitely more exacting, and are rapidly becoming affordable for many jewelers.

## Describing colored stones: More or less detail than diamonds?

We are taught that no two diamonds are identical (obviously we need more security than that knowledge, thus the use of laser inscriptions to identify particular diamonds!). This quality of uniqueness is also true for colored gemstones, and probably more so in the eyes of the consumer.

One of the qualities of colored stones that is most appealing to jewelers is the difficulty consumers have in shopping based strictly on price. If your customer falls in love with a beautiful tourmaline in your store and it is priced reasonably (and even if it isn't), you have a very good chance of selling the stone with little competition from other jewelers for that particular sale. There will be other tourmalines to look at, and other jewelers will order goods on memorandum in an effort to duplicate the feeling your customer has for the one she saw in your store. But often there is a particular quality in a color that "speaks" to a customer, and once she as seen a stone whose color is appealing, she will not be satisfied with any stone but the one she saw orginally.

The qualities that make colored stones a unique sales opportunity, also make them a unique appraisal responsibility. Consumers buy colored stones primarily for their color. This obligates appraisers to describe that color accurately, thus facilitating the processing of a future insurance claim.

Color is best described in terms of ***tone, saturation*** or ***intensity,*** and ***hue***. Tone is simply a description of the gem's lightness to darkness —from very light to very dark. One of my GIA instructors once said, "Imagine what this gemstone would look like on black and white television. That will help you to visualize it on a colorless to black scale." Saturation, sometimes referred to as intensity, has to do with the strength of the gem's color—from very weak to vivid. Imagine a glass of water, to which you add drops of dye. At first the saturation (intensity) is very weak. With each drop, the intensity increases. The color (hue) does not change, it merely becomes more concentrated. Hue refers to the gem's color—purplish red, greenish blue, etc. So, "medium dark (tone), strong (saturation) purplish blue (hue)" might describe a tanzanite, for example.

These three elements are the basics of color description. Other elements are important as well. As with diamonds, you will have to make decisions, appraisal by appraisal, as to how much information is necessary to properly identify the gemstone for insurance purposes. Some aspects of a gem's appearance are listed below for your consideration.

1. Transparency: Transparent, semi-transparent, translucent, semi-translucent, opaque

2. Clarity: Very lightly, lightly, moderately, heavily, or very heavily included
    If you use this terminology, it is advisable to add a few words to explain what your criteria were. For example, if you were to describe an amethyst as "heavily included," you might add in parentheses, "fingerprint inclusions and fractures are easily visible to the unaided eye." The description of a rhodolite garnet as "very lightly included" could also include in parentheses "minute crystals and needle inclusions, visible only under magnification—no inclusions visible to the unaided eye."

3. Polish or Finish: Poor, fair, good, very good, excellent

4. Symmetry: Poor, fair, good, very good, excellent. Note any important irregularities, such as an off-center culet, misaligned facets or facet junctions, bulges in outline or shape, flat lobes, shoulders, or sides.

5. Overall appearance: Color zoning, mottling (as in some jade), windows, other characteristics of growth, any irregularities in appearance.

6. Damage: Scratches, abrasions, nicks, chips

7. Phenomena: Color change (what are the colors, is the change weak, moderate, strong, etc.). Asterism, or star (How many rays? How is it centered, or how off-center is it? Are the rays straight? Are the rays consistent lengths?) Chatoyance, or eyes (similar criteria as for stars, including centering, straightness vs. waviness, brightness, consistency)

### Describing colored stone melee

Melee obviously requires a different approach than a main center stone. Apply some of the principles discussed in the section on describing diamonds, and you will find that common sense generally rules. For example, the rubies in a cluster ring might be described as follows: "The rubies are medium to medium dark, moderate purplish Red, and lightly included (no inclusions visible without magnification), with very good polish, and good symmetry." This paints a verbal picture of the rubies in one sentence. Any inconsistencies can be described in another sentence or two. For example, "Two rubies on the lowest tier are chipped, and one near the top of the ring is very heavily included, making it nearly opaque."

Under no circumstances are terms like "fine color" or "beautiful cut" acceptable appraisal terminology. Such terms do not provide anything close to the kind of description necessary to accurately assess a loss and provide a proper replacement.

This might seem like a lot of information to absorb, if you are not used to employing it in your appraisals. The habits you develop will determine how easy or difficult it is to describe colored stones and diamonds. Practice describing gems that are in your own inventory. If there are other people in your store who are interested in the subject, it is helpful to discuss and perhaps debate the proper manner in which to describe a particular gem. With a little bit of practice, the development of your own ordered procedures, and the use of worksheets (see Chapter 10, "A Matter of Form," for worksheet samples), it will become routine to provide detailed, accurate descriptions.

## Color description systems

The verbal color descriptions discussed in this chapter are very important because they convey an image of color to a lay person. Consumers and their insurance carriers have to be able to understand our descriptions, or part of the purpose of writing the appraisal is lost. But important colored stones warrant more exacting descriptive information—enter the color description system.

A good example is Gemdialogue™, originally created and still owned and supported by Howard Rubin. By laying color transparencies over one another, and adding grey or brown **masks**, it is possible to reproduce thousands of gemstone colors. You can choose the coordinates you judge to match the subject gemstone most closely, then record the information in the appraisal and your notes. GIA GemSet™, a set of colored, faceted plastic chips, is another tool that allows for detailed description of a gem's color. If you can find the exact or nearly exact match, simply record the number on the appropriate chip. Imagine that your clients and their insurance company are in litigation over a claim. There is some question about what color the lost gemstone was. You are hired as an expert witness. You take out your Gemdialogue kit, or other description system, recreate the color you recorded in your appraisal, and state, "Your honor, this is the color of the gemstone in question, as I recorded it at the time I rendered the appraisal."

This is the extreme case, and not likely to be a part of most appraisers' experience. But you are very likely to be asked to replace a gemstone you've appraised. And once again, by exercising some forethought and a conscientious approach to appraising, you can be a hero to your customer.

As with plotting, new technologies are poised to revolutionize the manner in which we record and attempt to duplicate gemstone colors.

## Photographs: Images that enhance your descriptions ... and your image

It is no less than astounding that anyone would write a jewelry appraisal (or any other appraisal for that matter) without including a photograph or photographs of each and every item described. Probably less than one out of fifty appraisals I have seen in the past several years contained photographs. The absence of photographs is just another symptom of the lackadaisical attitude most jewelers have taken toward appraisals.

Photographs contribute in a minor way to the expense of producing appraisals. Yet they contribute in a major way toward the smooth processing of an insurance claim. Most of us are not as observant as we would like to think. This includes our insurance replacement customers, who are almost universally unable to remember the design details of their jewelry. A photograph can eliminate hours of sifting through catalogs and store inventory searching for something that will make a satisfactory replacement. It is the responsibility of the appraiser to look ahead to the possibility that the appraisal will actually be used to replace jewelry. If you accept this responsibility, you have no choice but to include photographs in your appraisal.

Once again, decisions have to be made. Is black and white Polaroid photography sufficient? Are color Polaroids necessary? Should you move to the next level, using 35mm color? For most situations, 35mm color photography is recommended. Photographs that are more than adequate (in fact, they will be the envy of most appraisers!) can be taken without the expense of portable studio-type lighting and professional equipment.

The following equipment has proven to be more than adequate for nearly all appraisal situations for jewelers. Find a 35mm SLR (single lens reflex) camera that can be accessorized with a 90mm macro lens and ring flash unit. The lens should not be one of the macro zoom lenses, but a fixed, telephoto 90mm lens. This lens will allow you to focus so closely that a clear hallmark stamped inside the shank of a ring will be large enough in a 3" x 5" photograph, to easily identify.

A ring flash is a unit that actually mounts to the front of the lens, around its entire circumference. This provides very even, reliable lighting. A power pack rests atop the camera, attached to the hot shoe, and usually runs on AA batteries. To assure the most trouble-free and consistent photography, choose a camera with automatic light metering capabilities, and a dedicated flash unit that allows the camera to do all of the work regarding proper exposure.

Thanks to a very conscientious camera store employee, my photography frustration ended several years ago when I found what I consider to be a modestly priced but very efficient photographic setup. Look at the Olympus OM4 camera body, a 90mm macro lens (non-Olympus, is probably less expensive), and a dedicated Olympus T-10 ring flash unit. If you already own a 35mm SLR camera that accepts interchangeable lenses, check with the manufacturer to find out what accessories are available.

This is a good place for a reminder that photographs alone are not accurate enough to be relied upon to accurately replace a colored stone. Photographs are essential for design representation, and the equipment described above will certainly allow you to present impressive photographs. But always include verbal color descriptions as well. Then, even if the photographs become separated from the written part of the appraisal, your client will still have a detailed color description. Photographs do not take the place of descriptive information they supplement it. And once again, make sure your AID explains the limitations of photography regarding color reproduction.

Polaroid photography has improved dramatically in the past few years. For many, if not most, appraisal applications, Polaroid photography may be more than adequate. For diamond engagement rings, for example, when color is not an issue, this faster method will improve your turnaround time. Some appraisers use both 35mm and Polaroid formats, and juggle the two according to quality requirements, time considerations, and other needs.

It is important to realize that many insurance companies do not have the facilities or technology to store photographs. Insurance replacements are often crippled by the insurance company's failure to produce the only existing photograph of a lost item. With Polaroid prints, there is no negative. The insured might submit it with the original appraisal, assuming that it will become part of a permanent record. Recently, upon investigating the whereabouts of such a photograph, the adjuster found out and informed the replacement jeweler that the photograph had been thrown away, and that it was this insurance company's normal procedure to do so.

Some appraisers believe that because insurance companies do not always retain photographs, they are not important. "The insurance company doesn't want all of that stuff. They don't care, so why should I?" is a common refrain. The answer is simple. You are the appraiser. Your clients rely on you to understand and fulfill the requirements of professional appraising.

The advantage of 35mm photography is that you can retain negatives in the appraisal file, thereby ensuring that even lost photographs can be replaced. But whatever photographic format you choose, mount the photographs permanently, as an integral, paginated part of the appraisal report. **Instruct your clients to retain the original, color photographs,** along with the original appraisal, and provide them with a photocopy of the entire appraisal. Have a rubber stamp made that states "INSURANCE COMPANY'S COPY" or something to that effect. If you use a word processor, you can easily superimpose such wording on one copy of the document. This will remove any doubt about what should be retained, and which copy will be sent off, possibly to become irretrievable at a later date. Most insurance companies are very conscientious about preserving appraisal records, but things do get lost, particularly photographs. Consumers are very trusting in general, and will frequently submit the original appraisal unless you direct them to do otherwise. For added safety, make sure photo negatives (or copies, if you use the Polaroid format) are filed carefully for easy future reference.

### *Putting it all together...using what you have learned*

One of the commonly recurring complaints about appraisal courses is that they do not pull all of the information together at the end. Many students have said this could be accomplished by giving students the opportunity to actually create an appraisal report. Some recent efforts have been made to alleviate the problem, and wisely so.

At the back of this book you will find a sample appraisal report containing three item descriptions. This appraisal contains descriptions of different kinds of jewelry, along with some of the explanatory wording discussed throughout the book. This format does not develop instantaneously, and to copy it word for word will do you no good. It is the result of careful planning, a reflection of your ability and personal style. It can be easily revised and reorganized if you use a word processing program. This narrative format may be intimidating at first. But once you have created your basic document and refined its component parts, the act of putting the appraisal together is actually quite repetitive. Your clients will know what to expect, and be pleased with your consistency and professionalism.

# Appraisal Information Document
## SAMPLE

Insurance Appraisal,
Prepared for:

**Dr. and Mrs. Ross Stevens**
**918 Princeton Avenue**
**Harvard, New Jersey  08887**

### Purpose and Assigned Use

This Appraisal Report, covering twenty (20) jewelry item(s) is prepared for the purpose of estimating the retail replacement value(s) of the item(s) described herein, solely for the assigned use of obtaining or renewing insurance. *Use of this report for resale or other non-insurance purposes is likely to mislead potential buyers or other third parties.*

### Basis of Value

Values stated reflect replacement costs for comparable new items currently available or exact duplicates when indicated, except in the case of antique or period pieces or substantially, noticeably used pieces, in which case stated value is for replacement with a comparable used item. To be "comparable," a piece need not be an exact duplicate or even nearly a duplicate of the appraised item, but rather must be similar enough in vintage, style, utility, and condition to be able to be compared to it. As employed in this report, the term *retail* is defined as "a purchase made for personal use by the ultimate or final consumer."

The value estimate is based upon current information on the date of appraisal, and no representation is made regarding future or past value or with regard to other types of value, such as a price which may be realized by a private party in selling the item(s). The value(s) stated in this appraisal report are based upon replacement cost in appropriate retail markets, and it is important to note that an insurance company's actual cost of replacement may be lower.

Value estimates are derived from the appraiser's knowledge and ongoing market research, which may be supplemented by consulting appropriate specialists and/or through research in applicable local and national sources where similar items may be found. In analyzing available market information, consideration is given to design and design execution, quality, desirability, and period of manufacture.

### Sales Tax

Individual estimates of value in the appraisal do not include sales tax. A sales tax total calculated at the current local rate is usually stated with the total estimate of value at the end of the description portion of the appraisal. Due to the fact that Ralph Joseph Jewelers serves clients in more than one state and the sales tax rates vary, sales tax may not be included in every appraisal. *It is strongly recommended that clients contact their insurance agent or underwriter regarding sales tax as a part of the cost of replacement, in order to determine whether or not it is covered in the insurance policy.*

**Role of the Appraiser** *("Appraiser" includes both* Ralph Joseph Jewelers *and the undersigned)*

This appraisal report is not an offer to buy or sell the appraised item(s) at any price, nor is it a guarantee that the items are replaceable in the event of their loss. The stated value is not necessarily the same as the price at which the item would sell in this establishment.

Unless otherwise stated, the appraiser has no past, present or contemplated future interest in the appraised item(s), nor any other personal interest which would bias the report. Assignment of this appraisal and compensation for its performance are not contingent upon the values stated or the client's success or failure in the use of the report, nor is the estimated value based upon a percentage of stated value.

Unless otherwise stated, the property itemized in this appraisal was personally examined by the undersigned. If this appraisal report was prepared under environmental conditions which limit proper examination and evaluation of the item(s), the effects of such limitations on performance of the report will be explained.

Any additional consultation or future activity related to this appraisal, such as appearance at any hearing, deposition, trial, or pretrial meeting, will be billed by the appraiser at the rate being charged at that time, on an hourly basis. Partial or full payment may be required in advance if such work is required.

**Documentation**

Photographs included in this report are for the purpose of design representation and documentation, and should not be relied upon for accurate color reproduction, or for accurate representation of clarity, brilliance, or size. Verbal color descriptions of colored stones, and diamond description and grading systems and nomenclature employed are those developed and promulgated by the Gemological Institute of America (GIA). At the appraiser's discretion, "Gemdialogue"™ or other color description notations may also be used, in order to assist with color matching in the event of a loss.

A copy of the entire appraisal report, including notes and worksheets from which it was derived, will be retained in our files and held in the strictest confidence. It will not be released without the client's written consent unless we are legally compelled to provide access.

**Identification and Quantification of Materials**

Metal quality (i.e., 14K gold) is assumed to be consistent throughout a particular item, with that of the specific area tested and/or of the quality stamped or otherwise marked on the item, unless stated otherwise in the report. When testing is deemed necessary, it is either by the acid/scratch method, with an electronic testing device, or both. Either is generally accurate within 1 - 1.5 karat.

Unless otherwise stated, weights and measurements are estimates, based upon formulas and the use of measuring instruments as generally practiced and accepted in gemology and the jewelry appraisal profession.

Diamond grading is a subjective scientific procedure. Grades on the same diamond (particularly when mounted, and especially in yellow gold) may vary *slightly* from one professional, trained grader/appraiser to another, depending upon conditions of lighting, time allowed for grading, quality and accuracy of master (comparison) diamonds, and color and hue discrimination abilities of the appraiser. Unless otherwise noted, the appraiser color graded any diamond(s) described in this appraisal using a GIA graded and registered diamond color comparison set containing diamonds graded E, G, I, K, M, and V-W, compared to the subject diamond(s) under a daylight equivalent diamond grading light.

Due to the limitations created by the mounting, *diamond color and clarity grades are provisional*, and might be changed by the undersigned if graded out of the mounting at a later date. Because of these limitations, diamonds which are mounted generally will not be assigned a "flawless" clarity grade (even provisionally), "ideal" cut assessment, or "D" color (highest color grade on the GIA grading scale). If a diamond is accompanied by a laboratory report prepared by the GIA Gem Trade Laboratory and can be verified as matching the report, the undersigned may defer to the GIA assessment.

**Condition**

"New" denotes an item which is either brand new or shows a minute amount or no sign of wear or deterioration. All gemstones are secure unless otherwise noted.

"Normal wear" denotes an item which contains scuffing, scratches, or other wear which would occur in the regular use of an item of the approximate age of the subject piece. This designation generally indicates that the item might appear "like new" with light polishing and cleaning.

Other characteristics of condition may be described independently of the "normal wear" designation.

**Appraiser's Standards of Performance**

This appraisal has been prepared in accordance with the report writing standards prescribed by the *Best Society of Appraisers (BSA)*. A statement of the appraiser's qualifications appears on a separate page.

*This Appraisal Information Document* and the appraisal report, © Copyright 1996, Ralph S. Joseph and Ralph Joseph Jewelers. All rights reserved.

Ralph Joseph Jewelers

Respectfully submitted,

Ralph S. Joseph, BSA
Graduate Gemologist (GIA)

# *9* *Hyping the Typing*
## Generating the Document

"Why haven't you finished the appraisal on the gold rope chain yet?!"

Generating the physical appraisal document can be a nuisance, particularly to the solo practitioner working without support staff. Independent appraisers working alone on a small budget, generally find the formatting, typing, and assembly of the finished appraisal to be the most frustrating and inefficient part of their business.

Computers and word processors have made the task much more efficient. The technology available today is mind boggling, even compared to what was available just a few years ago. Failure to take advantage of that technology is, plain and simple, a mistake. One appraiser recalls using an antiquated word processing program, one that had not been supported by any company for several years. He stayed with that program for three or four years longer than he should have, for fear of not being able to understand something more advanced.

The time lost as a result of his fear of the unknown will never be recovered. But the important lesson will endure. Always look for ways to streamline your production process without sacrificing quality. A small initial investment of time, such as that required to learn new software, will ultimately pay for itself many times over. You will improve overall quality, both of the content and cosmetic aspects of your appraisal reports.

No doubt many readers are still hand writing appraisals on a pre-printed form. Let us not belabor that issue, except to urge you to enter the twentieth (okay, twenty-first) century. Handwritten appraisals are inefficient and unprofessional, and perpetuate the public's perception of appraising as a free, "gift wrap" kind of service.

The next level is obviously the typewriter-generated appraisal. Once again, it is time to move on. The use of a typewriter demonstrates a desire to create a more professional looking appraisal document, but the flexibility and speed required to generate truly professional appraisals are not available with the typewriter. An attempt to conform even marginally with the suggestions made in this book, using a typewriter, will result in a dependence upon static forms and boilerplate wording. You will find this cumbersome and frustrating.

Level three is the word processing typewriter. Better, to be sure, and not long ago probably more than adequate. Technology has left this device in the proverbial dust. The serious appraiser has to think about the competition and what technology they utilize. Simply put:

**If you do not own a computer, buy one now and learn how to use it!**

For the professional appraiser, the benefits of a sophisticated word processing program cannot be overstated. With word processing and the speed and efficiency of today's personal computers, procedures that were complicated and time consuming several years ago can actually be pleasant. The Appraisal Information Document discussed in Chapters 7 and 8 can be created in several forms for different kinds of appraisal assignments. At the touch of a button (okay, a *few* buttons), you can add appropriate changes of name, date, and wording as necessary. Almost instantly, your saved document has been customized for the assignment at hand.

Computing also allows you to create and save other elements that you might not use in every appraisal report. Glossaries, explanations of diamond grading or other nomenclature, gem treatment disclosures, and other addenda can be saved, customized, and merged with your descriptive information quickly, easily, and neatly. Computers also allow you to create graphs simply by entering data. A graph can make your narrative descriptions and explanations come to life. Without a computer, graphs are unwieldy and time consuming to create.

Worksheets like those samples presented in the previous chapter are easily adaptable to computerized word processing. After you have created your own worksheets to conform to your particular style and format (also made easier with computers), you may be able to use them as templates, requiring only that you fill in the necessary information. At the very least, the manual entry of descriptive information is made easier by using a standard format.

If you have a secretary or typist putting your appraisals on paper for you, the transfer of worksheet records to a computer word processor is fast, simple, and almost guaranteed to have a mistake-free result. Such "no brainers" are a welcome part of any appraiser's day.

If you ever have occasion to work with other appraisers on a larger assignment, you will find the computer-driven word processor indispensable. Not long ago I teamed with another firm on the appraisal of the entire contents of a large cathedral. The vast majority of the content—art, antiques, furniture, and antique silver—were out of my area of expertise. I had to hire the other firm to supplement my work. As the contracting party, I was asked by that firm about my preferences with regard to the type style, layout, and other cosmetic elements of the appraisal. By trading diskettes and samples, we were able to coordinate our efforts from afar, and eventually we produced a cohesive-looking appraisal that appeared to have been generated by one company. In fact, the work was performed by three different individuals, and the two hundred-plus page appraisal was quite impressive in its consistency.

Perhaps the most mysterious method for producing appraisal reports is the appraisal program designed specifically for jewelry appraisers. There are several on the market, and despite differences in the philosophies of their creators and general design, they seem to have one element in common. The driving force behind them all seems to be the need to convert data into a formal document, without the user manually typing all of the information and narrative as we do with word processors.

One program I experimented with took raw data (diamond measurements, color, clarity, metal quality, etc.) and placed it into sentences, actually creating an entire narrative description of the item from data entered into pre-programmed fields on the screen. The disadvantage of that system was that it forced me into the narrative style of the program's creator. Admittedly that was several years ago, and the system might have changed. But the purpose of this chapter is not to analyze specific programs. It is to illustrate what their potential is, while also pointing out possible limitations that must be examined.

If you decide to seek out appraisal software, look for flexibility. The need to generate both narrative descriptions (i.e., the Basic Worksheet page in the next chapter, with a summary description of the item) and lists (diamond grading reports, for example) should guide you in your search for the right program for your needs. The flexibility to arrange and rearrange information at will is paramount, and anything less will inhibit your ability to perform at your peak.

One significant area where the computer can save you time is gemstone weight estimation. If you are tired of making calculations by hand while examining set gems, a good software program can relieve you of that burden. The gem's dimensions and any weight adjustment percentages you decide on can be entered into fields on the screen, and the computer will then estimate the weight(s) for you. If you do a lot of your gemological examination in the presence of your clients and like to discuss weight estimations with them, this tool can be very helpful. It is often necessary to save weight estimation calculations for a time after the client has departed, in order to speed up the examination process and get on to the next client. With the use of an on-site software program, the appraisal can be completed, or nearly so, in the presence of your client. Impressive to your clients? Yes, indeed.

Laptop and notebook computers now allow you to be portable and efficient. You can move one of these small marvels just as readily as you have previously moved your worksheets or note pads. But be warned—once you enter this high-tech world, you will probably never want to turn back. Years from now you will be amazed when you look back at the primitive manner in which you produced appraisals before you computerized.

There are some caveats, however. Many programs determine value for you, not requiring the thought processes that separate professional appraisers from the rest of the pack. Generally these programs allow the user to override the automatic value conclusion, and it is strongly advised that you take advantage of that option. Certainly, instant access to colored stone and diamond pricing guides can be helpful. But the same warnings expressed in

Chapter 5, "So What's It Worth?" apply to the use of computerized appraisal programs. For example, what if someone offered you a gemstone pricing grid built into the program? Once you had described the gemstone(s), the program would pull prices out of the grid, apply a pre-set markup (determined by you, of course), and state a value. Presto! Instant value. As attractive as this might seem, it is a dangerous temptation.

This is not to say that price guides are to be avoided. They can be very helpful, and in fact can be a valuable backup to your own research. Guides that are reputable and based upon actual market research can be invaluable in your pursuit of accurate market information. Just be wary of anything too automatic. Bottom line, you still have to assess the gemstone in question, and make a judgment based upon your own research and knowledge of similar material.

Appraising is a thought process and always will be. Computers can help us to automate our clerical work, but not our valuation responsibilities. Values assigned in your appraisals should be well thought out before you make that written commitment. Computers are limited—they only know what we tell them. It is imperative that what the appraiser tells the computer comes from the appraiser's knowledge of the marketplace and ongoing or specific market research. Any price guides included with a program, if reputable and based upon actual market research, can be valuable tools. But also stay in touch with the market, and use your ongoing research to assess value based upon your own observations.

In your excitement about the time a computer will save you, remain cognizant of what price guides and grids can and cannot contribute to the appraisal process. Relying on them blindly can cause problems. Using them as they are defined—as guides—can benefit your clients, and you.

## *Mounting photographs*

Assuming of course that you have decided that photographs are essential to your appraisals, there arises the question of how best to present them. Some appraisers like to mount the photograph immediately adjacent to the item description. Others prefer to number them and place them immediately after the body of descriptive information for all items in the appraisal.

Word processing technology allows you to do either with ease. You may find that having to calculate the space required for photos adjacent to each item description will be time consuming and frustrating. If this is the case, placing photographs in order at the end of the descriptive section is acceptable, and easy. You can create a basic form for the photograph pages, simply changing the name and page numbers at the top of the page. Number the photographs by typing the numbers on the page itself, or create tiny, laser-printed labels which can contain your logo (if you want to get fancy!) and individual item numbers. The stickers can be applied to a corner of each photograph, thereby eliminating the need to lay out the page at all.

Mounting photographs can be as easy or as difficult as you like. So why not make it easy? Of course the ultimate in ease is to not mount them at all. But this does a disservice to your client. One appraiser simply sets the loose Polaroid photographs into a pouch in the folder used to present the appraisal. Loose photographs often get lost if retained by your client. Polaroid photographs are irreplaceable because there are no negatives. Thirty-five millimeter photos are replaceable only if the negatives are retained and accessible to you or your client. If you supply photos loose, you will almost certainly be asked at some point to produce additional copies. This is trouble for you and your client, and is unnecessary if you plan well.

So whichever format you choose, mount photographs. My favorite product, made by the Liquid Paper company, is Dryline™. Be sure you buy the permanent adhesive, *not* the removable kind. This permanent adhesive comes on a roll that fits into a hand-held dispenser. You just roll the adhesive onto the back of the photograph, press it into place, and you're finished. After a few minutes the adhesive becomes quite permanent, but I have noticed that in the first few seconds you may be able to straighten or even cleanly remove a photo.  Don't press too hard until you're sure the photo is in the right place!  Dryline™ is available at most large office supply stores.

Many less efficient methods are still employed, but seem unnecessary with such a clean, easy-to-use product on the market.  Just for comparison's sake:  The old fashioned stick-on corners can still be found—you know, the kind you used for your Brownie Starmite camera photos when you were a kid.  One appraiser demonstrates a system that employs a steam iron.  With the iron, he tacks dry transfer tissue to the back of the photo, then heats it to stick it to the page.  Three  secretaries at one large jewelry firm regularly struggle with a glue stick.  The result is not too bad, but it seems like a lot of work considering the alternatives available.

If the Dryline™ product is unattractive because you really hate mechanical "stuff," the Parker photo album people make adhesive strips that contain a dry glue similar to that in the Dryline™ dispenser.  They are available at some photo specialty stores, in packages containing several sheets of the strips.  You peel them off the page, stick them to the back of the photograph, and peel away the strip, leaving only the glue.  Then you affix the photograph to the page.

There are also spray adhesives available from camera stores.  These are particularly messy, however.  You will have to spread your photos out on a newspaper or other large sheet of paper, spray all of the backs of your photos, mount them, and carefully fold up and discard the paper.  It works, but it is a lot of trouble.

Lamination of the entire page is another option.  This protects the photograph and is permanent and secure.

Experimentation will lead you to the system that works best for you.  But whatever it takes, mount photographs permanently into your appraisals.  Advise your clients to keep the original appraisal with the color photographs.  Provide them with a complete photocopy, including photographs.  Stamp it "INSURANCE COMPANY COPY" or something to that effect, so it is clear which you intend for them to keep for their records.  If the insurance company's copy is ever lost, your client will be very grateful that he or she has retained the original.

## Now you are really in a "bind.  How do you package the appraisal?

There are several theories about the best manner in which to present the finished appraisal.  Some prefer to bind the report with a plastic spine.  The "Velo-bind" system is very effective.  It consists of front and rear covers, joined to the pages via a pair of binding strips that are affixed through a series of holes along the left side of the page.  A machine that lets you perform this procedure manually but effectively costs less than $500.00.  An electronic version costs nearly double that.  Unless you bind several appraisals a day, the larger expenditure is probably not warranted.

The thinking of some appraisers is that binding helps to protect your work from tampering by an unscrupulous client or third party.  However, even the seemingly permanent Velo-bind is easily cut open with a special blade, and rebound just as easily with no sign of tampering.  One appraiser tells a story about a former employer who changed figures in her reports, then reissued them!  So binding of any kind (short of a hardbound book) should not be seen as the cure for tampering.  But it does make an impressive presentation.

There are also do-it-yourself spiral bind systems available.  Although I have not used them myself, they look nice and may be your preference.  In either case it is probably not necessary or even advisable to bind the insurance company's copy of the appraisal.  Insurers may need to make internal copies, and are likely to take the binding off anyway.  Binding the consumer's copy will give that original a sense of permanence, and is a good idea.

Another approach keeps the practical use of the appraisal in mind.  Consider a folder with your logo on the front, and two internal pouches.  On one side you can insert the original, and on the other the insurance company's copy. If you are not concerned about slowing down the tampering process, this system may be the best. Each copy can be inserted loose, without any binding at all. One advantage of this method is the ease with which you can make changes. For example, your client may alert you to a typographical or other error that must be corrected. The folder presentation precludes your having to unbind the report to make the correction. Updates are easier as well. Pages are easily replaced and addenda can be mailed out and inserted easily by your client.

Sometimes a three-ring binder is appropriate, particularly with very large appraisal reports. The aforementioned two-hundred-plus page appraisal of the contents of a cathedral was delivered in such a binder, with a customized cover, and each page of the appraisal set into a plastic cover. This protects the pages long term, will make the appraisal usable in a practical manner, and is very flexible for updates or changes as the cathedral client makes new acquisitions or divests itself of some of the old ones.

Whatever you decide about the packaging and presentation of your appraisals, they should be typewritten at the very least, and ideally, laser printed for maximum cosmetic appeal.

If you present your work professionally, you are sending a message that you care. And after all, your clients' jewelry means a lot to them or they would not consider insuring it. Show them that what is important to them is important to you. Generating cosmetically appealing appraisals is just another small way in which you can send that message.

# 10

*A Matter of Form*

## Pre-printed Forms and How They Can Help

*Good form has its rewards.*

M uch of the "busywork" associated with appraising can be streamlined through the use of pre-printed forms and worksheets. Many jewelers do not want to become involved with appraisals because of the labor-intensive nature of producing and organizing the appraisal documents. This chapter provides the foundation for the creation of forms that will work for you.

The samples included in this chapter have been used in my appraisal practice, in varying versions over the years. They are included in order to guide you, with the understanding that they will most likely have to be modified to suit your particular needs. If they work for you just as they are, the forms can be ordered as a set from the publisher, along with permission to reproduce them.

### *The Take-In Form*

The take-in form should be designed to complement the pre-assignment interview. Much of what will be explained during that initial consultation can appear in the take-in form. If your attorney advises the use of a contract for services, consider the convenience of printing it on the reverse side of the Take-In Form.

The form should include spaces to fill in the following information:

### Section I

1. Client's name, address, and daytime and evening phone numbers.
2. Special instructions, such as a mailing address or fax number of an insurance agent or other individual to whom your client would like the appraisal sent.
3. The take-in date.
4. The expected, estimated, or required completion date.
5. The type of appraisal (i.e., insurance, charitable contribution, estate tax, etc.).
6. Further explanation regarding the assigned use of the appraisal.
7. Page number of the take-in form (for multiple items that require additional pages,"Page 1 of 3").
8. The total number of items listed on the form.
9. The agreed-upon fee, range of expected fee, or maximum fee to be charged.

### Section II

1. A brief description of each item to be included, numbered.
    a) (Note: For organizational purposes, you will find it helpful to list the items in the order they will appear in the appraisal. That way you will have begun to organize the jewelry in a logical manner from the start. You might want to establish groupings, perhaps separating men's and women's jewelry, and within those two categories, grouping diamond jewelry, gold jewelry without gems, colored stone pieces, pearls, watches, etc.).

# APPRAISAL TAKE-IN [This form is not an appraisal]

Client's Name_____     Take-In Date _____

Address_____     Type of Appraisal _____

_____     Explanation _____

Home Phone   (   ) _____-_____     _____

Business Ph   (   ) _____-_____     Page _____ of _____ pages

Special Instructions_____     Total Number of Items _____

_____     ESTIMATED FEE $_____

_____     Estimated Completion Date_____

| ITEM # | DESCRIPTION/DAMAGE | REPAIR INV. # | CLIENT'S DECLARED VALUE |
|--------|--------------------|---------------|-------------------------|
|        |                    |               |                         |
|        |                    |               |                         |
|        |                    |               |                         |
|        |                    |               |                         |
|        |                    |               |                         |
|        |                    |               |                         |
|        |                    |               |                         |
|        |                    |               |                         |
|        |                    |               |                         |
|        |                    |               |                         |
|        |                    |               |                         |

**Note: Client's declaration of value is for insurance purposes, and does not constitute a delcaration of value or quality on the part of Ralph Joseph Jewelers or the Appraiser.**

## COMPLETE AT TAKE-IN

Repairs approved on #     _____

I have read and understand the *"Agreement and Authorization for Services, Terms and Conditions"* on the reverse side of this form.

Client's Signature     _____

Take-In by     _____

## COMPLETE AT PICK-UP

Date delivered _____

Delivered by     _____

I have received _____ my jewelry

_____ the completed appraisal report.

Client Signature_____

## *Agreement and Authorization for Services, Terms and Conditions*

**This appraisal report is presented subject to these terms and conditions unless any or all are expressly set aside in writing.**

1. The appraisal is performed under the assumption that the client named therein is sole owner of the item(s) being appraised. The appraiser does not investigate any representations made by the client as to ownership.

2. The stated estimates of value are based upon the appraiser's best judgment and opinion and are not a guarantee that the item(s) will realize said value if sold by the client. No representation is made as to past or future value and the appraisal is not an offer to buy, broker, or liquidate the property.

3. Value conclusions are valid only for the specific purpose and assigned use stated. The appraiser and/or RSJ Jewelers will not be responsible for the appraisal or its content if it is used for any other function (i.e., an insurance appraisal being used as a sales or promotional tool, or submitted with a tax return).

4. Possession of the appraisal report does not carry the right of publication and it may not be reproduced without written permission from RSJ Jewelers. The appraisal should not be relied upon by anyone except those named for its use, and then only in its entirety.

5. The appraisal report including all notes, worksheets, photographs and negatives is the property of RSJ Jewelers. The client named herein is licensed in its onetime use, for the purpose and function stated, by virtue of payment of all required fees to RSJ Jewelers. The appraisal report is copyrighted in its entirety by the appraiser whose signature appears on the report, and by RSJ Jewelers, and acceptance of the report is acknowledgement thereof.

6. Mounted stones are evaluated only to the extent that the mounting, in the sole opinion of the appraiser, permits examination. Unless otherwise stated in the appraisal report, all weights of mounted stones are estimates, calculated using formulas and measuring instruments as generally practiced and accepted in the jewelry appraisal profession.

7. Any indication by the appraiser as to the condition of the appraised item(s) shall not be deemed to be an all-inclusive listing thereof, nor does the appraiser or RSJ Jewelers assume any liability or responsibility for any defects not listed.

8. It is understood that any colored stones described in the appraisal may have been subjected to a possibly undetectable color enhancement process or other treatment. Prevailing market values incorporate these precesses, which are commonly practiced and accepted by the gem and jewelry trades. Gem descriptions will indicate enhancement(s) only when they are detectable and impact value considerations.

9. Any appearance of the appraiser in court or at any other hearing regarding the appraisal report or related matters will be made only if reasonable notice is given, and upon payment in advance for each day of such service at a rate to be determined by the appraiser at that time.

10. Client agrees to allow RSJ Jewelers to perform the usual testing procedures for gemstones and metals. Client agrees that liability of RSJ Jewelers for loss, theft or breakage is limited to the time in which the jewelry is in our possession, and is limited to the cost of repair or replacement, solely at our discretion, but in any event not to exceed the value stated by the client on the front of this form.

11. RSJ Jewelers will not release the appraisal report to anyone other than the client named herein without permission from the client, unless we are legally compelled to do so.

**All disputes including the validity of this agreement shall be settled by arbitration pursuant to an arbitrator to be appointed by the American Arbitration Association.**

2. A cross-referencing of any repair ticket numbers.

   a) Your appraisal business is the perfect vehicle for building your repair department. You have to closely examine items to be appraised, looking for damage or excessive wear. When you discover either, suggest that the repair be performed prior to the appraisal examination—explain that the appraisal will then state the item's condition as good, rather than noting wear and tear or damage. When you record the repair ticket number on the appraisal take-in form, you will create a backup record of the repair order.

3. The client's declaration of value.

   Be sure to note that the client's declaration of value is not indicative of your opinion of the item's value. It merely serves as a basis for determining the level of liability in the event of a loss, should it occur while the item is in your possession. A statement to that effect is advisable, along with notification that you have the option of replacing the item with one of comparable or better quality (as opposed to simply paying out the value declared by your client). The implementation of such a payout varies from state to state. Generally, a payout will occur only if the loss is due to the appraiser's (jeweler's) negligence. Again, state laws vary. Some require that the jeweler carry insurance to cover the customer's property, and some do not. Some laws require that the jeweler inform the client as to the absence of insurance. Know and follow your state's laws in this regard.

## Section III

1. The name of the employee who took in the jewelry.

2. The client's signature, acknowledging the information contained on the form. This can include a statement such as "I have read and understand the contract for services on the reverse side of this form."

3. The item numbers from the take-in list that are approved for repairs (another backup for your records and the customer's decision to make repairs).

## Section IV

1. The date the appraisal and jewelry are delivered, or two dates if they are different.

2. The name of the employee who delivered the jewelry and/or the appraisal.

3. The client's signature, acknowledging receipt of the jewelry and appraisal.

   a) It is helpful to have two check-off boxes, one for the jewelry and one for
   b) the finished appraisal. It is very common, particularly with a multi-item
   c) appraisal, for some or all of the jewelry to be picked up before the appraisal is completed. The check-off boxes are helpful in keeping accurate records of this activity.

A retail sales associate took in a large diamond ring for cleaning and appraisal. The customer was a prominent physician in the community, a gentleman who had traded heavily with the jeweler in the past. During the cleaning process the diamond shattered. The pieces were given to an independent gemologist who happened to be working in the store that day. He identified the "diamond" as Cubic Zirconia.

The take-in form had identified the stone as "diamond, five carats-plus," with no limitation or declaration of value. The customer was due back before the end of the day, and the salesman was terrified of the confrontation that would take place. Just before closing the customer arrived to pick up the ring. The nervous salesman explained what happened, and that the stone was CZ.

"I knew that was too nice a gift. I just knew it couldn't be a diamond, despite what they told us." The salesman breathed a sigh of relief. No doubt he will be more careful with his take-in procedures in the future!

## Worksheet Forms

Worksheets seem to be the never-ending bane of the jewelry appraiser. Unlike many other forms of personal property, the individual components of jewelry often have to be described in detail separate from the general description of the item. For this reason I developed worksheets that include all of the information I might want to include in a description. When an item is less complicated or the assignment requires less detail, I have the option of skipping sections of the worksheets.

Samples of worksheets that have been used successfully for some time are included at the end of this chapter. Worksheets should be developed with an eye toward the orderly, easily-interpreted recording of gemological information obtained during examination.

The worksheets shown here may seem complicated at first. But as Chapter 9 on generating the document notes, it is important to follow a uniform format so that secretarial personnel can easily interpret the data on your worksheets. With practice and modification to suit your needs, you will find the worksheets simple and easy to use. At the same time, you will be able to provide detailed, fairly consistent item descriptions in your appraisals.

This particular worksheet format was designed in response to feedback I received during my early days as an independent appraiser. Most were from clients who actually wanted to read the item descriptions (it's true, sometimes your appraisals will be read!) and found them difficult to follow. People in the insurance industry had also commented on occasion that they found the item descriptions complicated, when they were really looking initially for just a summary of the item's identity and description. I adopted "summary" as the operative word, and designed the worksheets to provide the summary first, then gradually work into the detail.

All of the accompanying worksheets are designed to be easy and fast to fill in, while remaining understandable for any secretary who can read your writing (sorry, but dealing with illegible handwriting is beyond the scope of this book). You will notice that many descriptive elements can simply be circled. These samples are just that, and the worksheets you design for your own use may contain even more basic information for checking off or circling. Rather than go into detail about the content of each worksheet, let us look at how they can be combined to create a cohesive item description.

As a first example, we will look at a diamond engagement ring, with a center diamond flanked by two baguettes and four small round brilliants. The BASIC DESCRIPTION worksheet can be used to establish the summary description of the ring, including metal quality, design description, diamond weight totals, signature or trademark, manufacturer if known, and the total weight of the ring. Please note that the basic summary should be typed in all capital letters to distinguish it from the more detailed information on the worksheet. In this way, a concise summary of the worksheet information is easily found and quickly read.

Next, go to the SECONDARY DIAMONDS worksheet. Here you can go into detail about the dimensions, cutting style, color, clarity, and other aspects you wish to note. This particular worksheet has room for two sets of melee. So you can handle the baguettes and rounds separately after having summarized their aggregate weight (or separate totals, whichever you prefer) on the BASIC DESCRIPTION sheet.

Lastly, turn to the DIAMOND GRADING worksheet. This is designed for the main diamond in the ring. It can contain the minimal information noted on most independent laboratory grading reports, or more as you prefer. The box at the top, asking whether or not the diamond has been plotted, is merely to alert a typist or secretary that the plot exists and room must be made for it with the item description.

The worksheets for SECONDARY GEMSTONES (color) and PRINCIPAL COLORED STONE can be used in combination with the three described previously. In any event, it is advisable always to use the BASIC DESCRIPTION worksheet in order to establish a consistent style of describing items. This will be appreciated by both your clients and insurance underwriters and claims adjusters, who are generally looking for the basic information before delving into the details.

Watches seem to be particularly problematic for appraisers. They are not as generic— for lack of a better word—as other kinds of jewelry, particularly when we talk about vintage watches. Many appraisers I have spoken to are at a loss as to just what information is important. How much detail is enough? This may vary from watch to watch. Sometimes a watch can and should be opened to record information about the movement. There are times when a watch will not be opened because to do so would require your sending it out—your client may prefer that you not do so. If this hindrance has a significant effect on your ability to value the watch properly you should either pass on the assignment, or consider a contract clause that absolves you of liability, based upon your client's refusal to have the case opened. As always in legal matters, consult with an attorney. If value cannot be properly determined without opening a watch to examine and inspect its movement, and you are not allowed by the client to do so, it is often advisable to simply turn down the assignment.

In any case, the WATCHES worksheet was designed to include any and all information that might be relevant to insured value. As always, how much information is filled in will be determined by the individual circumstances of the appraisal, the nature of the watch involved, and perhaps the wishes of your client.

The CULTURED PEARL NECKLACE/BRACELET worksheet form is self explanatory. One note of importance, however. With the creation of pearl grading master sets over the past several years, this form might be simplified even further. If you are using a master set for pearl grading and descriptions, you may be able to include the entire range of quality in each category, then simply circle the appropriate grade or description.

The idea behind including the worksheets in the book is straightforward and practical. Many appraisers still work from notes scribbled on a legal pad, simply because they never have the time to sit down and design a worksheet that would free their memories from the burden of every element to be included in an item description. By developing forms that suit your style, you will save time and eliminate the frustration felt by many of the unfortunate folks who have had to interpret and then type or word process our often unintelligible "gemo-babble!"

CLIENT: _____

ITEM # _____ : _____

ONE ITEM ONLY: _____

---

{LADY'S * GENT'S} {CONTEMPORARY * TRADITIONAL * VINTAGE (CIRCA _____)}

{14 KARAT YELLOW GOLD   *   18 KARAT YELLOW GOLD   *   STERLING SILVER   *

PLATINUM   *   14 KARAT WHITE GOLD   *   18 KARAT WHITE GOLD   *

OTHER _____ }  _____

_____

_____

_____ , WITH _____ FINISH,

OF { CAST  *  HAND FABRICATED  *  MACHINE MADE  *  OTHER _____}

CONSTRUCTION,                     CONTAINING

                                                                          Approx.

_____ _____ WEIGHING _____ CARAT TOTAL,
Number            Gem type

                                                                          Approx.

_____ _____ WEIGHING _____ CARAT TOTAL,

                                                                          Approx.

AND _____ _____ WEIGHING _____ CARAT TOTAL;

THE _____ IS STAMPED "_____ "{(_____
                                                                    Manufacturer's name

_____) * (MANUFACTURER NOT IDENTIFIED). *

AND NO MAKER'S MARK IS APPARENT *}. THE TOTAL WEIGHT OF THE _____

IS _____ DWT. ( _____ GRAMS).

CONDITION:  New - Normal wear;_____

---

Prelim. Value (RJ only)_____ ESTIMATED RETAIL REPLACEMENT VALUE: $_____
Comments:

CLIENT: _____     **WORKSHEET - SECONDARY DIAMOND(S)**
(can be used for two sets of diamonds, i.e., rounds and
baguettes in the same ring)

ITEM # : _____ (continued)

The _____ are / is _____ ,
shape and cut

measuring approximately _____ x _____ x _____ mm  - in diameter - through - _____ x _____ x _____ mm.

They are approximately_____ color and _____ clarity,

with _____ polish and _____ symmetry.

The _____ are / is _____ ,
shape and cut

measuring approximately _____ x _____ x _____ mm  - in diameter - through - _____ x _____ x _____ mm.

They are approximately _____ color and _____ clarity,

with _____ polish and _____ symmetry.

Comments / Further description: _____

_____

_____

_____

Client _____

# DIAMOND GRADING WORKSHEET

| ITEM # _____ (continued) | Plotted?  Yes ____   No ____ |
| --- | --- |
| | [Internal use only] |

## The Center Diamond

Diamond examined:                     Mounted _____     Loose _____

Shape and cut:                        _____

Diameter (rounds only 0.00 - 0.00mm)  _____ mm

Length x width (fancy shapes 0.00 x 0.00mm)  _____ mm

(Estimated) Depth:                    _____ mm

[ESTIMATED * ACTUAL] WEIGHT:          _____ carat

COLOR:                                _____ *

CLARITY:                              _____

[Estimated] Depth percentage:         _____ %

Estimated table percentage:           _____ %

Girdle thickness:                     _____

Culet size:                           _____

Estimated crown angle:                _____ degrees

Estimated pavilion depth:             _____ %

Polish:                               Poor/Fair/Good/Very good/Excellent

Symmetry:                             Poor/Fair/Good/Very good/Excellent

Fluorescence:                         _____

Cut:                  Cut grade or Class _____  ( _____ )

Comments / further description:  * (use asterisk with split grades to denote which grade the value
conclusion is based upon; i.e., "stated value is based upon G color," when "G-H" is the stated color grade)

_____

_____

_____

CLIENT: _____        **WORKSHEET - SECONDARY GEMSTONES (COLOR)**
                                          [for use with colored melee and/or lower grade commercial
                                          center stones when appropriate]

ITEM # : _____  (continued)

_____

The _____ are _____ ,
                                       shape and cut

measuring approximately ____ x ____ x _____ mm  through ____ x ____ x ____ mm.

They are _____ , _____ ,
          transparent / semi-transparent / translucent / semi-translucent / opaque          tone (very light through very dark)

_____ , _____ , and
saturation  (weak, moderate, etc. through vivid)          hue (i.e., slightly bluish purple, yellowish green, etc.)

_____ included (                                    ).
clarity (very lightly through very heavily)          (explain: eye clean, easily eye visible, etc.)

Polish:  Excellent  *  Very good  *  Good  *  Fair  *  Poor

Symmetry:     Excellent  *  Very good  *  Good  *  Fair  *  Poor

_____

Comments / Further description: _____

_____

_____

Client: _____

Item #:_____ (continued)    **WORKSHEET - PRINCIPAL (MAIN) COLORED STONE**

_____

The center _____ is a _____,
                                                    shape and cut

measuring approximately _____ x _____ x _____ mm. It is _____,
                                                         transparent / semi-transparent / translucent / semi-translucent / opaque

_____ , _____ ,
tone (v. light through v. dark)        saturation (weak, moderate, etc. through vivid)

_____[Color description system Notation:          ],
hue (i.e., slightly bluish purple, yellowish green, etc.)

and _____ included.
      (explain: eye clean, easily  eye visible, etc.)

Polish:        Excellent * Very good * Good * Fair * Poor

Symmetry:    Excellent * Very good * Good * Fair * Poor

Window: Approximately _____ %  Extinction: Approximately _____ %  Brilliance: Approximately _____ %

_____

Comments / Further Description: _____

_____

_____

_____

_____

Client:_____    **CULTURED PEARL NECKLACE / BRACELET**
                                                          **WORKSHEET**

**[Terminology should be changed to match your pearl
master set, if you use one]**

Item #: _____

LADY'S {SINGLE STRAND  *  TWO STRAND  *  THREE STRAND  *  OTHER _____}

{CHOKER  *  PRINCESS  *  MATINEE  *  OPERA  * } LENGTH CULTURED PEARL
NECKLACE /BRACELET, AS DESCRIBED BELOW.

Length including clasp:              _____ inches

Number of pearls:                    _____

Size:                                _____mm

Stringing:                           Knotted throughout  *  Partially knotted  *  Strung without knots

Shape:                               Baroque  *  Semi-Baroque  *  Off round  *  Slightly off round  *

                                     Mostly round  *  Round

Color / overtones:                   _____

Uniformity of color:                 _____

Luster:                              Dull (very low)  *  Low  *  Medium  *  High  *  Very High  *

Nacre thickness:                     Very thin  *  Thin  *  Medium  *  Thick  *  Very thick

Surface characteristics:             _____

                                     _____

Matching                             Poor  *  Fair  *  Good  *  Very Good  *  Excellent  *

Total weight of necklace / bracelet: _____ grams

Condition:                           _____

Clasp: _____

       _____

Comments: _____

**ESTIMATED RETAIL REPLACEMENT VALUE: $**_____

**WATCHES (Pg. 1 of 2)**

ONE ITEM ONLY: _____

CLIENT: _____     ITEM # _____ : _____

{LADY'S * GENT'S} {CONTEMPORARY * TRADITIONAL * VINTAGE (C.     )}

{14 KARAT YELLOW GOLD * 14 KARAT WHITE GOLD * PLATINUM *

STERLING SILVER * 18 KARAT YELLOW GOLD * 18 KARAT WHITE GOLD *

TWO TONE ____ KARAT YELLOW GOLD AND STAINLESS STEEL *

STAINLESS STEEL * OTHER _____}

_____ , WITH _____ MOVEMENT,
Kind of watch - wrist / pocket / pendant                    quartz/mechanical/automatic

BY _____ , MANUFACTURER'S STYLE NUMBER

_____ , SERIAL NUMBER _____ .

━━━━━━━━━━━━━━━━

The case is

_____
Describe case

AND_____
      describe bracelet or attachments (chain, bow, etc.)

_____

_____

The dial is _____ , with _____ hour markers,
                  color/texture/other                      arabic / stick / roman # / other

{a _____ second hand * no second hand},
      sweep / subsidiary / other

and _____ hands, signed "_____

_____ ."

## WATCHES (Pg. 2 of 2)

Additional signatures or markings include the following:

Case back outside: _____

_____

Case back inside: _____

Movement: _____

Clasp or buckle: _____

The total gross weight of the watch, { including  *  excluding } the movement, is

_____ dwt.  (_____ grams).

Condition: _____

_____

Comments: _____

_____

Preliminary value estimate — for internal use only - do not include in appraisal _____

**ESTIMATED RETAIL REPLACEMENT VALUE: $**_____

**(Add the following statement to the appraisal if your value conclusion reflects a commonly available discount.)**

**Note:** The estimated retail replacement value stated reflects a discount of ____% off the manufacturer's suggested list price of $_____. Discounts in this amount are commonly available in the normal marketplace for the watch described herein.

# 11

## *The Stated Value is Accurate, so What else Matters?*

## **The Basics of Insurance Replacement**

"Whaddya mean you can replace it for $3,000?
I had it insured for $6,000!"

**"L**oss Settlement.  *We have the option of repairing or replacing the lost or damaged property.  Unless otherwise stated in this policy, covered property values will be determined at the time of loss or damage.  We will pay the cost of repair or replacement, but not more than the smallest of the following amounts:*

    *a. the full amount of our cost to repair the property to its condition immediately prior to the loss or damage;*

    *b. the full amount of our cost to replace the item with one substantially identical to the item lost or damaged;*

    *c. any special limit of liability described in this policy; or*

    *d. the limit of liability applicable to the property."*

Of the entire insurance policy, this wording is probably the most important for the appraiser to be aware of and understand.  This excerpt is quoted precisely from a major insurance carrier's policy, and you will find similar language in every replacement policy, comprising approximately ninety percent of the personal property insurance market.

It is commonly believed by jeweler/appraisers that as long as the stated, or estimated value is accurate, the appraiser's responsibility has been met.  In fact, the dollar figure included in the appraisal is often less important in the real world than the description is.  A closer look at this wording and its ramifications is important.

The second sentence states that values "will be determined at the time of loss or damage."  For obvious reasons, we are concerned with a total loss.  After all, once the item is gone, there is no way to accurately describe it.  Everyone involved is totally dependent upon the description contained in the appraisal, the photograph(s) included (or not, as is too often the case), and the insurance company's interpretation of that information.

Insurance claims adjusters generally are not jewelry experts.  Insurance claims offices retain the services of replacement vendors, whom they rely upon to help them interpret losses, and "time of loss..." values.  Replacement specialists are frequently called upon to work backwards; that is, to look at the two- or three-sentence, sketchy description of the lost item, correlate that with its stated value, and work from the value backwards to fill in the gaping holes in the item's description.  This becomes a hit-or-miss situation, with the policy holder usually compelled to identify several items before a satisfactory replacement is achieved.

Assuming as we have so far that the appraisal is inadequate, determining the value at the time of the loss becomes something of a guessing game.  The replacement specialist must determine the value of an item by literally creating a description, rather than having the simple but critical luxury of working from an existing, detailed description.

Why in the world would any jeweler want to put cherished customers in this uncomfortable position?  A comprehensive, detailed description included in every appraisal of every item will assure your client that in the event of a loss, the nature and quality of what is being replaced, will be abundantly clear.

Item "*b*" states **"... to replace the item with one substantially identical to the item lost ..."**  This presents another version of the same problem.  Simply put, how can we possibly replace an item with something substantially identical to a mythical item of which we have no detailed description?  By failing to describe your client's jewelry properly, you may be subjecting them to a less than equitable future insurance settlement.  At the very least you will increase their stress level at a time when they have already sustained a loss of property and, along with it, their peace of mind.

## How Replacements Are Made

In order to discuss the problems caused by inadequate appraisals, we should be familiar with basic claims procedures. There are essentially two kinds of insurance policies available to consumers. The names vary, but for simplicity's sake we will refer to them as the "Full Value," "Agreed Value," or "Cash Value" policy, and the "Replacement" or "Actual Cash Value (ACV)" policy. The former kind of policy is just as its name implies. The value is agreed upon at the inception of the policy. When a loss occurs, that previously agreed-upon value becomes the cash settlement amount for the claim.

In this chapter, and generally throughout this book, we are not dealing with agreed-value policies, but with replacement or ACV policies. These kinds of policies give the insurance company the right to replace, or at least shop for the replacement of, the lost item. Shopping for a replacement helps the insurance company to determine the ACV of the item at the time of loss. The policy will state this clearly. Yet, most policy holders are surprised upon sustaining a loss when they are not simply issued a check for the appraised amount. One claims adjuster once said to me, "Our policy holders need to understand that their policy number is not their bank "PIN" (personal identification number). We are not the Automatic Teller Machine."

When a loss occurs, the policy holder informs his or her agent, or in some cases the insurance company directly. Shortly thereafter, a claims adjuster, sometimes called a claims representative, is assigned to the case. The insurance company is obligated to return the policy holder back to his or her original position prior to the loss. The adjuster's job is to make the policy holder "whole" again by implementing the replacement clauses in the insurance contract. Up to the limit of the company's liability (the appraised value of the item), the insurer will spend whatever is necessary to meet its obligation. This, once again, means replacing the item with one substantially identical, or as it is sometimes known, *"of like kind and quality,"* to the item which was lost.

A note before continuing. Most homeowners' policies have very low limits for jewelry which is not covered with special riders or floaters. Items which are listed in a floater are commonly referred to as *scheduled* items. The limits for non-scheduled items are often as low as $1,000.00. In virtually all cases, a deductible applies as well. This might be as little as $250.00, but is frequently $500.00. This amount must be paid by the insured when there is a loss, and the insurance company pays the excess up to the policy limit for valuable articles. Some companies offer upgrades on this kind of general coverage. Not to imply an industry standard, but upgrades are typically $2,500.00 to $5,000.00, and sometimes more. But regardless of the monetary limits, the property is often covered only against fire and theft, or the named perils in the general homeowner's policy. Most upgrades, however, also add perils such as mysterious disappearance (i.e., "I don't know what happened to my ring. It just disappeared, and I don't know where or when.") and others that are not named in the basic policy. "All risk" coverage is nearly always provided with a special rider for jewelry and/or other valuables. In addition to the standard homeowners' coverage, this includes such perils as mysterious disappearance and others which may not be included in the basic homeowners' policy.

A recent appraisal (generally less than a year old, or possibly even six months) must be submitted to the insurance company in order to secure the all risk coverage we will be discussing. The appraisal is submitted to an underwriter along with the insurance application. The underwriter will decide whether or not the property will be insured by the company for the dollar amount specified in the appraisal document.

Unfortunately, underwriting requirements are not at the level that a professional appraiser would consider to be acceptable. Anyone involved in the insurance replacement business knows that the sketchy, two or three line item description is still being accepted frequently by insurance companies. Although such descriptions are inadequate should the replacement scenario occur, they are accepted by underwriters quite regularly.

Some jeweler/appraisers feel that the answer to the question of insurance appraisal standards is simply to find out what the insurance industry wants. One letter to the editor of *National Jeweler* magazine queried, "What does the insurance industry require?" The letter indicated that finding the answer to that question would establish what we as appraisers should feel obligated to provide for our clients. As appraisers we are responsible for the accurate, complete, objective assessment of our clients' cherished jewelry. Ethically we should provide a document that will result in the very least amount of research when a loss occurs. If an underwriter will accept less, so be it. We are not underwriters or underwriting police, but appraisers. To adapt to what another industry requires or establishes as its guidelines might very well be to shortchange our own clients. You cannot hurt your clients by providing appraisals written to a standard that exceeds what their insurance company requires.

Jewelers often ask why the insurance companies do not simply go back to the selling jeweler in order to attain proper documentation. After all, the jeweler sold the piece and is therefore intimately involved with the it. One insurance company representative answers the question this way: "*1*. We insure property; we do not determine value. We accept our policy holder's estimate, which is often obtained through an appraisal. *2*. We are concerned about accusations of price fixing."

### Out In The Cold

Imagine that you just purchased a new automobile, with a factory installed AM-FM radio. You happily drive your new vehicle all summer, listening to music exclusively on the FM band. Then winter comes. You are caught in a blizzard and switch to the AM band, to the Weather Station in your area. You find out that the AM radio doesn't work. The dealer just wanted to get the car sold and off the lot, and figured you'd ask about the radio when you brought the car in for service. Everything else worked, and that was good enough.

But you bought the car assuming everything would work properly, including the radio. You relied on the dealer to deliver a car that would meet your needs. And when you really needed that AM radio, it didn't work.

Could you be leaving your clients out in the cold if you skimp on your appraisals? And if you do, will they be cursing you the way you might curse that car dealer when the AM radio doesn't work?

Too often, appraisers do not think ahead about how (or even IF) the appraisal document will be used in the event of a loss. If you haven't had the experience, imagine how it might feel to have something you treasure stolen from you during a burglary of your house (a violation of your space and psyche), or worse yet, an armed robbery (a violation of your person). Wouldn't you want the replacement of that stolen item to be as painless as possible? Your appraisal clients deserve the consideration you would expect if you were in their position.

So much for the jeweler/appraiser who fails to think ahead. There are also those who very carefully *do* think ahead—but project incorrect or downright untruthful information into their plans. This is particularly so when we look at jewelers' practices for documenting the merchandise they sell.

When the words "appraisal" or "appraising" appear in quotes in this section, it is for a reason. Chapter 2 on documenting what you sell makes clear the fact that a record of an item you sold in your store is not, by definition, an appraisal. And so, the quotes.

One jeweler once told me that his rationale for "appraising" every item he sells at 50% or more over its selling price, was that "the insurance company routinely will pay only 75% of appraised value." He continued, "Nobody is hurt but the insurance company, and I don't care about them."

There are gaping holes in this philosophy. Imagine a common item that regularly sells for around $1,000.00 in local stores. You sell it for that amount, and routinely "appraise" it at the point of sale, stating a value of $1,500.00. Assume for the moment that the item description is accurate and truthful. If you can regularly sell the item for $1,000.00 to consumers, there is a very good chance that an insurance company can buy it for $700.00 (or possibly a bit more or less) ... if not from you, then elsewhere.

Suppose the policy holder has had other losses and is tired of having to worry about her jewelry. Or perhaps she is not ready to replace right now. She informs her claims adjuster that she wishes to cash out. After receiving a replacement quote of $700.00 from its replacement vendor, the insurance company will offer that amount as a cash settlement for the loss (That $700.00 figure is an example only. It may be that the insurance company's cost is $900.00, in which case $900.00 will be offered as the cash settlement for the loss.

In any event, the offer may be substantially less than what you stated as the item's value in your point of sale "appraisal" document. Your client will initially think she's being cheated by her insurance company—but only until the policy language is explained to her. She will then begin to wonder why you overstated the value of the item, which caused her to pay premiums on that mythical value. She may also begin to wonder what else you lied about. And the impact would be even greater if the figures were $10,000.00 and $15,000.00.

Try to explain that you overstated value using that misinformed jeweler's "75% of appraised value" assertion. Seventy-five percent (75%) of $1,500.00 is $1,125.00, which exceeds your selling price. The chances are very slim that an insurance company will offer more than the selling price. The numbers just don't add up, as the saying goes, and you are the ultimate loser, because your client will wonder if you can be trusted.

Some jewelers react to this discussion with belligerence. "Okay," they say, "it seems we should appraise jewelry at or very near wholesale prices, when we know that our customer's policy allows the insurance company to replace the property. That way, no excess premiums will be paid." This sounds good on the surface, but understand that premiums are based upon the insurance company's known cost of replacement, as compared to typical appraised values. In other words, the premiums would be higher if the insurance industry's cost of replacement became a higher percentage of appraised value. So if appraisals are routinely written using wholesale or near wholesale values as the basis for insurance coverage, insurers will be paying nearly 100% of appraised value for replacement (assuming that the stated values are accurate at this level), and premiums will go up. So nobody benefits from manipulation of a system that, if everyone cooperates, will work fairly well. Cooperation, after all, is a major theme of this book.

Most homeowner's policies contain a statement such as: "**Concealment or Fraud.** *This entire policy will be void if, whether before or after a loss, you have intentionally concealed or misrepresented a material fact or circumstance relating to this insurance.*" This bit of overkill is intended. The overstatement of value is a plague on the appraisal profession, and even more acutely on the jewelry industry in general. If you are ever contemplating an overstatement of value on an item you sold, keep this in mind. As stated in Chapter 2, your client's failure to disclose the material fact that your appraised value is overstated by 50% could void the terms of the policy in the event of a loss. Appraising is a service. You do not serve your clients by putting their future rights in jeopardy.

Example: A jeweler sells an engagement ring and provides the following insurance documentation. "Ladies' diamond engagement ring, 14 karat gold, the round diamond estimated at 1 carat, H/VS. Estimated replacement value for insurance, $5,600.00." The item actually sold for $3,800.00. This kind of documentation is extremely common, and is generally not accompanied by a photograph. Some jewelers routinely "appraise" their own merchandise as high as double the selling price! Of course, many questions arise. "What does the ring look like?," is an obvious one. "Is the diamond set with prongs? How many? Or is it bezel set? What is the rest of the ring like? How much does it weigh—is it substantial, or very light weight? How is the cut of the diamond? Is the table percentage 70%? Is it 57%? Is the girdle polished? Is the crown overly steep or shallow? Does the diamond have any characteristics that would help to identify it in the event of its loss and eventual recovery by police? Is the diamond fluorescent?" And so it goes, on and on. The questions would increase and expand for a more complicated item, yet the description often does not.

Now to complicate matters further. The jeweler who wrote this description also misrepresented the diamond's quality. In fact, the diamond was actually K color, and $SI_2$ clarity, and really only weighed 0.97 carat. As you will recall, the actual selling price was $3,800.00. When a loss occurs, the insurance company calls its trusted replacement vendor for a quote. The vendor, not knowing whether the lost diamond was $VS_1$ or $VS_2$ clarity quotes for both, based upon "1 carat," and H color as stated. The quote for the higher clarity grade is $5,900.00, and the lower is $5,700.00. These quotes are generally based upon lower markups than would be offered to the retail consumer, so we will assume that is the case here.

Both are higher than even the overstated value used in the point of sale document. And both quotes are substantially higher than the original purchase price. So what happens now? The policy holder is actually underinsured based upon what she thought she had. This can only arouse her suspicion toward everyone involved. The replacement vendor will state that there is insufficient insurance to cover the loss. The claims adjuster then has to make a decision about whether or not to pay the full limit of the policy.

Sometimes an insurance company will cash out the full limit (in this example, $5,600.00). In this case, the insured is not hurt financially. But she has been informed that even the insurance company, with its multiple sources, cannot replace a diamond of the represented quality within the terms and monetary limit on the policy. This arouses suspicion that might very well be directed at the appraiser. And often the insurance company, upon seeing that even with their discount they are not able to actually replace the diamond, will check further before electing to cash out for the limit ($5,600.00) of the coverage. In some cases they will ask for the original sales receipt. That sales slip, which shows a selling price of $3,800.00, will prove that a material fact was withheld at the inception of the insurance policy. This could void the coverage, and the claim might not be paid at all. A justifiably angry consumer might very well decide to sue the jeweler who fooled both her and the insurance company with a misleading point of sale "appraisal." At the very least, the insurance company in this example has been given the upper hand in negotiating a settlement of the claim ... and the appraisal put them in this position!

It is not uncommon for a policy holder to report a loss, then find the item while the claim is being processed. Sometimes the item is found after a replacement has been made. When this occurs, the insurance company often gives the insured the option of retaining the new, replacement item. Imagine the insurance company's reaction when its salvage expert examines the original item and discovers the discrepancy between what was represented in the inaccurate appraisal, and what the item really is. This cannot be good for the appraising jeweler's relationship with that insurance company.

Jewelers who engage in this kind of practice may think they are fooling insurance companies into paying out larger settlements. In fact, claims adjusters usually know which jewelers in their area engage in this practice, and will never allow them to be a replacement source. Additionally, they will begin to question any document with that jeweler's name on it. Although they will probably not accuse the jeweler specifically, they may be openly critical of the appraisal and outspoken about the problems it has caused with settling the claim accurately.

It should be pointed out that claims adjusters are not looking for trouble. In fact, they are motivated by heavy case loads to settle as quickly and easily as possible. But they are also responsible for settling claims accurately, and that means for both the insured and for their employer—the insurance company.

Some jewelers are convinced that by withholding information in an appraisal, they will have a better chance at being the replacement source if a loss occurs. After all, if there is no information in the appraisal, where can the insurance company go for more details? The thinking is that the adjuster will call the appraiser/jeweler for that information, allowing the jeweler to offer to replace the item. This may work in the short term, but once again, adjusters are very sensitive to problems caused continually by the same jeweler. It does not take long for jewelers to get a reputation—good *or* bad—and the long term harm will far outweigh the short- term profit, which may be an illusion in the first place.

## *The Jeweler as Insurance Replacement Vendor*

Insurance replacement is a balancing act. You must constantly weigh your need to make certain profit margins against your desire to build this part of your business, if that is your goal. Working with documentation that is often lacking in both detail and accuracy of what little information there is, you must satisfy the needs of both the policy holder and the insurance company.

The policy holder has to be satisfied because if they are not, you will not see continuing business from their insurance company. The insurance company has to feel that, in terms of both price and service, they have been treated fairly and honestly, and they have paid the right price for the merchandise. Part of that chemistry results from the policy holder's reaction to your service and the replacement itself.

Even if you do not pursue insurance replacement as a part of your business, there may be times when you are prevailed upon to deal with an insurance claim. This generally occurs when a customer who trusts your establishment tells the insurance company that he or she prefers to replace through you. This conversation may occur even before you have been made aware of the loss.

The purchase may have been made elsewhere originally, and you will therefore have to deal with another jeweler's appraisal, or point of sale "appraisal." Having certain basic information at your disposal will assist you when these claims come your way.

It is easy to become frustrated over point of sale "appraisals" that are inaccurate, incomplete, or otherwise lacking. Frequently the jeweler who prepared the document will be someone you know, or have heard of. You may see the same "H/VS" diamonds that, based upon the documentation, you suspect are really $K/SI_2$. In any event, it is imperative that you maintain a positive attitude with both the customer and the insurance claims adjuster.

There will be the temptation to say, "Based upon the value stated, and what I know about this jeweler, there is no way that the diamond was really H/VS as stated. It was probably a K/SI." But bad-mouthing your local competitor can land you in court defending yourself against a defamation suit, and that makes you sound as though you're doing business at that jeweler's level. Rather, you might say, "Based upon the item description and the value stated, your policy holder is underinsured."

If you are speaking to the policy holder, you will likely be pressed for more information. You will have to carefully explain that the item described is just not available for the amount stated. Let the customer and claims adjuster draw their own conclusions about why that is.

The adjuster will figure out what that jeweler is doing. If not on this claim, over the next several claims their practice will become clear. The customer is likely to go back to the jeweler and ask why there is insufficient coverage. The jeweler may offer to make the replacement at or below the insured amount. The replacement by such a jeweler is likely to be misrepresented just as the original purchase was, since this will be the only way to make a replacement without losing money. This is a very real possibility, and one that is difficult to combat. This customer, by now wary of representations made by this jeweler, may double check the quality of the replacement item carefully, thereby revealing the jeweler's chronic misrepresentations.

Initially it is annoying to lose a replacement in this situation. But take heart. Insurance companies eventually know who the perpetrators are, and this only creates more opportunities for the honest jeweler to establish long term, profitable relationships with the insurance industry.

The insurance replacement arena is fraught with twists and turns. The "what ifs" abound, and it is not the intention of this book to deal with every scenario involving disreputable jewelers. It is mentioned and discussed here briefly in order to alert the reader to some of the difficulties caused by the dishonest jeweler who uses abuses the appraisal process to gain an advantage in the marketplace.

The information you provide—or fail to provide—does impact your clients. You do them a disservice by doing just enough to get past an underwriter. You also do them a disservice by withholding information in a mistaken effort to gain by providing a replacement in the event of a loss. Your job as an appraiser is to provide the information necessary to make a fair and accurate replacement in the event of a loss. To do less is unfair to your clients, and without them your business would not exist.

## The Basic Stages of Insurance Replacement: Step by Step

1. You receive a request by telephone or fax, for a replacement quote. This may be the result of the requesting adjuster's familiarity with your business, or at the request of a consumer who wishes to replace through you.
   - Hint: Keep worksheets by the telephone, and use them to record all important elements of the claim from its inception. As one insurance company memo state, "If it isn't in the file, it didn't happen."
2. If an appraisal has been provided with the request, examine it carefully and make notes to help you zero in on the specific item(s) you will be replacing.
   - Hint: The first thing you should do is make sure that the stated value makes sense, based upon the item's description. A one carat $E/VS_1$ diamond with a stated value of $2,500.00 is a red flag with the words "WASTE OF TIME" printed on it.
   - Hint: If that is the case, remember to state that the policy holder has insufficient coverage for the item described, rather than question the integrity or competence of the appraiser.
   - Hint: Don't rely completely upon price sheets or lists when making quotes. It is helpful sometimes to call a vendor who will have the item you need, so that you are quoting on a specific available diamond or other item. Even if that item is sold before you request it, you know your quote was accurate and most likely repeatable.
3. Ask during the first communication with the adjuster, if the loss is scheduled (insured by a rider or floater in addition to the basic homeowner's policy). If the loss is not scheduled, there will be basic limits of coverage, and a deductible amount payable by the policy holder. The insurance company will pay the balance, up to the limit of the coverage.
   - Hint: When there is a deductible, plan to collect it yourself—before you special-order anything or deliver in-stock merchandise. This assures you that you do not have to bill the policy holder later, and is a convenience to the insurance company.
   - Hint: Most non-scheduled losses will not involve an appraisal. This means working with the policy holder to determine what was actually lost, then quoting the price to the insurance company for approval. The determination of the loss can be facilitated using photographs, the policy holder's drawing, and looking through catalogs and/or your inventory.
4. In either case, work closely with the policy holder if necessary to determine just what the item was. "Bedside manner" is critical. This person has sustained a loss of property and possibly a sense of security. Your attitude can make or break the replacement (versus a cash out, which will not benefit you at all, unless the policy holder returns to shop with you at a later date, which does not occur). Many if not most cash outs do not result in the replacement of the jewelry, but in the policy holder's paying off a debt or taking a vacation. Unless you own a travel agency, you will want to encourage replacement.

**5.** If you have not done so already, provide a quote to the insurance company for the item(s) chosen. Explain to the policy holder that you must obtain the insurance company's approval before releasing the merchandise to them. If you have already provided an accepted quote in advance of meeting with the policy holder, you may be in a position to release the merchandise with nothing more than a signature. Once you have the release and authorization signed, you are essentially assured of payment by the insurance company.

   • Hint: The release and authorization states that the policy holder has received the new or repaired merchandise, is happy with the replacement or repair, and therefore authorizes their insurance company to pay you. Have an attorney assist you with the development of the form, or see if the insurance company has its own version. Sample wording can be found at the end of this chapter.

**6.** Fax or mail the invoice and release to the claims adjuster. It is very rare for an insurance company to take more than thirty days to pay on a claim.

**7.** As soon as possible, provide insurance documentation for the new item. Some insurance companies even require that you provide such documentation before they will pay your bill. As discussed in the chapter on documentation of items you sell, the written document you prepare should contain full disclosure.

   • Include a statement disclosing that you sold the merchandise to the insurance company as a settlement of Claim Number _____.

   • Note that the insurance company generally pays less than your normal retail price (assuming that this is the case), then state the retail price for which you recommend that the item(s) be insured. One appraiser has suggested openly that appraisers are ethically obligated to provide both the common, typical retail selling price for an item, along with the *insurance company's cost of replacement*. This seems absurd, however, in that insurance replacement is not a consistent, trackable market in and of itself. Values stated in this regard, therefore, could not be reliable. Many items replaced for insurance claims are not as represented, making hearsay data highly irregular and unreliable. Additionally, margins fluctuate dramatically, depending upon the professionalism and integrity of the replacement source, resulting accuracy or inaccuracy of the replacement, covered amount as compared to jeweler's actual cost (some claims are processed with a markup as low as 10%, others are sold at keystone or more), and other variables that come up on a claim-by-claim basis. The jeweler who has just made a replacement certainly knows how much the insurance company paid, but that is in this one case only. Another replacement service would probably have charged a different price. And if this suggestion is in the name of full disclosure, should the jeweler's *wholesale* cost then be obligatory information in the appraisal as well? No, because it is not relevant to the task of securing insurance coverage. The only thing in this discussion that is relevant is that the insurance company's cost of replacement is likely to be less than the retail replacement value stated, because insurance companies are volume, discount buyers. This or similar wording can be inserted into the AID for your client's edification.

   • You may have just witnessed the difficulty faced by a consumer who was forced to rely upon an incomplete or inaccurate appraisal. You can ensure that he or she will not have to do so again by providing a complete, accurate description including photographs.

   • Your inventory reference number can be very helpful to you and the consumer, as well as the insurance company, if you are ever called upon again to replace the item.

### *Forms you should develop and maintain*

- A quote form, with space for all essential information, including the claim number and any other pertinent facts.
- A dated release that states clearly that the policy holder is satisfied with the replacement or repair, with a brief description of the item or service, authorization to pay you directly (rather than paying the policy holder, whom you would the have to collect from), and any other information you deem appropriate.
- A worksheet you can keep by the telephone, to be used to record all important elements of the claim from its inception.

The intricacies of insurance replacement make it an exciting and potentially lucrative aspect of the retail and appraisal businesses. The steps outlined in this chapter are basic, and it is important to note that each can branch off into other scenarios. The core of insurance replacement is service and attitude. If you approach each claim with the attitude that "I will replace this item," you will find that insurance companies and their clients are likely to follow your lead, and everybody wins.

# INSURANCE REPLACEMENT QUOTATION FORM

**To:** _____

**Attention:** _____     **For Immediate Delivery**
**Please**

**Fax: (        )** _____

**Date:** _____

**Claimant:** _____

**Claim Number:** _____

<u>**REPLACEMENT QUOTE**</u> (*Valid for 30 days only*)

**ITEM DESCRIPTION**                                              **REPLACEMENT**
**COST**

## Release and Authorization of Payment

I hereby acknowledge that the repair or replacement of my (as described below)

_____ resulting from the damage to or loss of same,

which occurred on or about the _____ day of _____, 19___, has been performed to

my complete satisfaction, and I hereby authorize the _____ Insurance

Company to pay _____ Jewelers, (city, state), directly for the full / partial

(circle one) settlement of my jewelry claim covering the item(s) described herein.

      [describe item(s) and damage if applicable]

_____

_____

_____

_____

In consideration of payment, the named insurance company and _____ Jewelers are
hereby discharged and forever released from any and all claims or demands under
the claim referenced below, relating to the said damage and/or loss of the aforementioned
item(s).

Policy Number: _____    Claim Number:_____

Insured Print: _____    Insured Signature: _____

Date:_____

# RALPH JOSEPH JEWELRY
## INSURANCE REPLACEMENT CLAIM WORKSHEET

Insurance Company:

Claims office location:

Adjuster:

Phone/extension:

Insured name:

Address:

Phone number, home:

Phone number, work:

**CLAIM NUMBER:**

NOTES

---

First contact from:    Adjuster        Insured        Agent

Insured expecting our call?:    Yes        No

Insured wishes to replace?    Yes        No    [If "No," explain below]

_____

_____

_____

Scheduled Loss:    Yes        No            Coverage limit:

Non-scheduled Loss:    Coverage limit aggregate $        Coverage limit per item: $

Deductible: $

---

Item(s) description: _____

_____

_____

_____

Documentation available? Appraisal ❑    Photograph ❑    Other_____

APPOINTMENT?  YES  NO    DAY/DATE/TIME/WITH_____

# 12

*Bottom Line, Does it Add to My Bottom Line?*

## Organizing and Selling your Appraisal Services

*Do I really want to add to <u>this</u> bottom line?*

M y Uncle Chuck, a retired jeweler, had an interesting way of putting things. Often when I asked why he did not give in to a customer's request for a lower price on a piece of jewelry, he would say that it was "no fun" to sell something for too little. The message was clear. And if business isn't fun in that way, why bother? Appraising is so labor intensive that it is particularly subject to this line of thinking.

There are several keys to making appraising a profitable department in your store, including initial setup of the department, organization of files and records, selling the service both one-on-one and in marketing to the general public, and networking with other appraisers. The latter may be the most important for you, particularly if you choose not to be your own appraiser and do not want to have one on staff.

In a June 1995 *National Jeweler* article, Bill Bevill, an Oregon jeweler who at the time employed four American Gem Society Certified Gemologist Appraisers (CGA), spoke about the advantages of using outside independent appraisers rather than having his staff take on the task. "It's a critical area," he said, "and we demand that our salespeople reach [the CGA] level of expertise. But they still don't appraise eight hours a day. [Our appraiser] has a much better feel for the pulse in that area. I put staff where they're most valuable, and I'm perfectly happy to use a gentleman like [our appraiser] for my day to day appraising." Bevill went on to say that he was careful to choose a truly independent, highly-trained appraiser. That choice being properly made, Bevill noted, "We couldn't save any money or generate any more business by moving appraisals in house. I see it like payroll—my bookkeeper could do it, but not as efficiently [as our payroll service does it]. I can't afford to have my staff be that highly trained [as our outside appraiser]".

Whether you are an appraiser, you employ one, or you wish to use an outside independent appraiser, the information in this chapter will apply. In order for your appraisal department to be profitable (that means fun—remember what Uncle Chuck said!), it must be taken seriously and organized and marketed properly.

### Setting Up Your Appraisal Business

To establish a serious appraisal department it will be helpful to envision the big picture first, which should include marketing brochures, sample appraisals to show to your customers, a filing system, a plan for building business, a fee structure, and of course, an appraiser.

It may seem easy to start doing appraisals, but because the process is both labor and paper intensive, organizing and setting up in advance will eliminate much frustration and wasted time. Decide how you will file appraisals, and develop a system for following up and suggesting periodic updates. Have brochures printed and ready to distribute to the very first customer who asks for more information. Have a fee structure sheet available for staff, so pricing will be relatively consistent. And above all, make sure the appropriate and necessary time is scheduled. Professional appraising is not an activity that fills in, between more important things. It requires time and concentration. Being organized will help on both counts.

### Organizing Records and Files

A good filing system will help you to find old appraisals quickly, and will generate more business by making follow-up simple. I suggest that each appraisal have its own file, regardless of the number of items. This section assumes that you do not archive all of your appraisals on computer. But even if you do, it's a good idea to double up with hard copies.

On the tab of a three-cut manila folder, record the information necessary to locate active files quickly. For security reasons, it is a good idea to use codes for names, with the addresses and phone numbers omitted from your copies. That way if reports are ever stolen, the thief will not have addresses to accompany the vivid descriptive information about your customers' jewelry. A simple coding system is best. For example, an appraisal performed for Joan Smith on July 14, 1995, can be coded, "JS071495." This system is convenient and effective. Most word processors allow eight characters for file names. It is unlikely that you will have two clients with the same initials, for whom you do appraisals on the same day. In these rare cases you can modify one record. A separate file, stored elsewhere, can translate the codes to names, including other pertinent information.

In the upper right hand corner of the file folder, preferably in red, write the month and year the appraisal was performed. This will allow you to quickly scan your file drawer manually if your records are not automated. You might be looking, for example, for all appraisals marked with the month of July, two or possibly three years back. You can easily pull those files and write letters suggesting that an update may be required. Even if you determine that the stated values are still sufficient, you will have made contact with your customer, and possibly brought him or her back into your store. It is also helpful to write the date on which you examined the jewelry somewhere near the top of the folder. That way you will always be able to tell at a glance which orders came in first, and perhaps which should have priority for completion.

In the file folder you will keep everything pertaining to the appraisal. Worksheets, photographs, negatives, and research materials will be conveniently accessible. Whether you are computerized or not, it is a good idea to maintain hard copies of every appraisal. At the very least the descriptive information should be kept in the file for quick reference. If you change your AID frequently as I do, you should be sure you can match the appropriate AID with each appraisal, at any time in the future. One appraiser suggests simply keeping a file of your AID versions by date, so you can match them chronologically with any appraisal. This reduces the amount of paper you produce, while still allowing the accurate reproduction of any report. The unwieldy method, of course, is to simply duplicate the AID and keep it with the file permanently.

Store files by calendar year, and within each year, alphabetically. At the end of December, move your active (current year's) files into a storage box. Depending upon your level of appraisal activity, you may be able to store up to two or three years' worth in one box. Until the time comes for an update, you will find that the older an appraisal file becomes, the less likely a client is to call asking you to refer to it. So move the previous year's work to a storage room, and keep your files fresh.

Some readers may find this material rather obvious, but I am including it because organization is so important. Some jewelers simply stack up appraisals on an unused desk until they become unbearably messy—then move them to a less conspicuous place. This process continues until the appraisals are discarded, moved to an even more obscure pile, or finally organized in a file. Until the latter takes place, these procrastinators face embarrassment or worse if someone calls inquiring about the specifics of an old appraisal.

## Selling the Service

As with any product you offer in your store, appraisals must be sold. That means they have to be suggested to as many customers as possible. If you have a successful repair department, you have the perfect opportunity to build an appraisal business. Every item of value is a potential appraisal. Anyone who takes in repairs should be trained to promote appraisals. "Mrs. Jones, this is a lovely ring. Do you have it insured?" is the kind of opening query that can easily result in an appraisal job. A common reply is, "I have homeowner's insurance." The salesperson must then be ready to explain that the basic homeowner's policy alone may not be adequate without a jewelry floater added to the policy. You can alert your customer to the need for adequate insurance, thereby generating appraisal business and perhaps making a friend if a loss occurs in the future—a loss that might *not* have been insured if you or a member of your staff had not cared enough to bring up the subject.

Once the appraisal assignment is secured, "Do you have other things that might need to be appraised for insurance?" is a logical question, one that often leads to a larger job. Although appraising itself is a science rather than an art, the art of selling appraisals is an important one to develop. This can be accomplished by developing written training materials, by making the selling of appraisals a part of your regular sales meetings, and through role-playing conducted by members of your staff who are particularly adept at selling appraisals. Usually the appraiser develops this talent most thoroughly, but others will also attain a high level of performance if you emphasize appraisals in your training program.

Following are some sample training materials to guide you as you develop your own training program. These examples may or may not suit your needs, but at least they will plant seeds. Whether or not those seeds grow and thrive will depend upon your level of commitment to your appraisal department's refinement and growth.

## PART 1: APPRAISAL TRAINING AND MARKETING

### *Selling appraisals one on one with customers*

Once you are happy with the way your appraisals look and read, prepare several samples and place them in strategic areas in your store. Make sure they are available for your staff, and that everyone is familiar with the contents of the appraisals. There is no more powerful selling tool than a physical sample of your work. When customers question your fees, it is particularly helpful to be able to present a beautifully typed and bound appraisal, complete with color photographs and plot diagrams. What better way to illustrate your professionalism?

The following questions and accompanying answers should assist you in discussing appraisal issues with customers. Keep in mind (and remind customers of this when appropriate) that we are not insurance experts or even advisors. Customers should be encouraged to contact their insurance agents or insurance carriers directly for advice and specific information. We are only alerting them about the importance of having insurance, and conveying some basic information about how claims may be handled in the event of a loss.

The questions that follow are commonly asked; being prepared to answer them will enable your staff to sell appraisal services effectively.

### *"Why should I have my jewelry appraised?"*

There is a good chance that your jewelry, either individual pieces or as a collection, has more value than you think it does. If this is the case, you might want to consider adding a jewelry floater, or rider to your homeowner's or renter's policy. This will give you specific jewelry coverage, generally without a deductible, and which usually protects you against damage and "mysterious disappearance," plus other perils which may not be covered by your basic homeowner's policy.

### *"But I have homeowner's insurance. Doesn't that cover jewelry?"*

Usually it does, but for a small amount minus a deductible. So if your policy provides $2,500.00 of basic coverage for valuables, with a $500.00 deductible, you may actually only have $2,000.00 of coverage. There may also be a clause which limits the *per item* coverage to $1,000.00 or a similar amount. This means you might not even be covered for the loss of one $1,500.00 item. Because this basic "valuable articles coverage" in homeowner's policies generally does not cover anything except theft and fire, separate, specific coverage can be worthwhile.

### *"Why are your appraisal fees so high? My old jeweler never even charged for appraisals."*

Appraisals that are prepared properly can be very time consuming. In addition to providing color photographs with every appraisal, we include highly detailed item descriptions, a "word picture" that makes identifying your jewelry relatively straightforward. This process takes some time, and is therefore a bit more expensive. Our appraiser is a professional, and appraisals are performed to professional standards. Professional appraising requires an appropriate background and education, which cost time and money, so we have to charge commensurate fees.

### *"Do I really need all of that detail?"*

Most insurance policies allow your insurance company to replace lost or stolen jewelry with items of "like kind and quality." Most appraisers incorrectly assume that if the stated value is accurate, the description is not important. On the contrary, the description is critical. If your insurance company is to replace an item with one of "like kind and quality," and if you are to feel confident that this has been accomplished, you must both be able to identify what "like kind and quality" is. This is not possible unless we properly describe the item in the first place. Once a loss has occurred, it is generally too late to reconstruct a description.

### *"Can you leave out the photographs to save me some money on the fee?"*

We believe in producing an appraisal product that, to the best of our ability, will protect you if you ever sustain a loss. Photographs are critical to the identification and replacement of a lost item, so by skimping on this critical element of the appraisal, we do not serve you. A few dollars saved now might cost you many times the savings later, so we feel obligated to maintain our high standards no matter what. We would rather lose the appraisal assignment than do a less than professional job.

### *If insurance replacement is a part of your business, you might add the following:*

As a replacement source for several insurance companies, we are very familiar with the difficulties involved in making proper replacements when appraisals are inadequate. Most appraisals are not sufficient, and unfortunately for the concerned parties (policy holders and their insurance companies), a great deal of guesswork is involved. The replacement of your treasured jewelry should not be based upon assumptions or descriptions you have to provide from memory. If you allow us to appraise your jewelry, you will have a detailed record which assures you that any professional jeweler will be able to make an adequate and proper replacement.

### *"I received an appraisal from the jeweler who sold me the piece, at the time of purchase. Is that sufficient?"*

That depends upon the quality of the appraisal. Many so-called appraisals written at the point of sale are insufficient to properly identify an item after it has been lost or stolen. In some cases, the jeweler selling the merchandise will specifically omit information so as not to be bound by it. This information may be critical to you if you sustain a loss. At the very least, you should disclose to your insurance company that the jeweler who sold you the item is also the appraiser. This alerts your insurance company to a conflict of interest, and having disclosed this, you have given them the opportunity to investigate further if they choose to do so before underwriting the risk.

Our appraiser would be happy to review your old documentation to determine whether the information in it is sufficient. We are busy enough with appraisals that **are** needed; we have no interest in selling you one that is unnecessary.

### *"Can you give me a verbal appraisal. I just need the value for my own knowledge."*

Appraisals, even verbal ones, carry with them a great deal of responsibility. Appraisals have to be written, so that they can be explained and defended if necessary. An appraisal that cannot be verified can prove detrimental to you and to the appraiser. Verbal appraisals are worth less than the paper they're not written on.

*Please note:* It is important for appraisers to understand the predicament that the verbal appraisal can put them in. In the future, your client might display selective memory; that is, they might recall only what serves them, or make alterations to what was said in order to achieve a particular end. If a client alters what was actually said, your ability to defend yourself is undermined. If you provide verbal appraisals you could find yourself watching a court deciding what actually occurred between you and the client.

There are exceptional situations that might warrant a verbal *consultation*. It is advisable to take detailed notes, or better yet tape record the session, with your client's permission. Make sure it is understood that you are consulting about a client's potential purchase, for example, but that this "is not an appraisal." You might be asked to compare two items. "Which is the better value," you might be asked. Again, it is acceptable to act as a consultant and to make qualitative and quantitative comparisons. Just be sure you have records that can be used to combat the "he said, she said, I said, you said" syndrome. Appraisals properly prepared, in writing, can be a valuable tool. Conversations that can be altered too easily with selective memory might come back to haunt you.

### *"How often should my jewelry be reappraised or my appraisals updated?"*

Depending upon the nature of the jewelry, every two years is generally often enough. However, the value of certain kinds of jewelry can be more volatile, and other items might not require updates for several years. We would be happy to review your appraisal every year or two to determine if an update is necessary. Some insurance companies require updates periodically, and will notify the policy holder when the update is necessary.

### *"Tell me about your appraiser. Is he/she a gemologist?"*

Actually, yes, but appraising is such that gemology is not enough by itself.
Our appraiser has extensive education in the methodology of appraising, and regularly lectures and publishes articles on the subject. In addition to being a Graduate Gemologist of the Gemological Institute of America, our appraiser:

*1.* Is a Certified Member of the International Society of Appraisers (ISA). This certification cannot be purchased, and takes about a year and a half to earn. It can only be earned through extensive course work, report writing, examinations, and professional development activities.

*2.* Is a frequent lecturer on the subject and has taught courses for his appraisal society.

*3.* Was a course reviewer for ISA's newly rewritten courses in 1994.

*4.* Created and co-hosted a live radio talk show about jewelry and appraising.

*5.* Writes a monthly column on appraising for a national trade publication.

*6.* Attends appraisal conferences and seminars on a regular basis, in order to stay current on appraisal issues.

*7.* Attends trade shows, auctions, and other industry selling events, in order to keep abreast of various market levels and situations.

---

**DO NOT BE BASHFUL ABOUT TOUTING YOUR QUALIFICATIONS. YOU CAN BE SURE YOUR COMPETITORS WILL NOT BE SHY ABOUT THEIRS!**

---

*"I think I'll shop around, and I'll call you if I decide to have the appraisal done here."*

Of course we would love to do the appraisal for you, but if you have decided to consider someone else, we can provide a list of questions we advise you to ask a prospective appraiser.

---

*1. Are your appraisals typewritten?*

*2. Does your appraisal contain a clause stating that you are not responsible for the content or any action taken based upon the appraisal?*

*3. Do you include color photographs of my jewelry?*

*4. Do you draw plot diagrams of important diamonds?*

*5. Have you ever had your color vision and hue discrimination formally tested?*

*6. Do you have any formal gemological education? Please explain.*

*7. Are you a member of an appraisal organization?*

*8. If so, are you certified or otherwise credentialed by that organization?*

*9. If you are, what were the requirements to achieve that credential or certification?*

*10. Do you have any formal appraisal (in addition to gemological) education? If so, please tell me about it.*

*11. Will I know before work begins exactly what the charges will be?*

---

The answers to these questions will provide you with a professional profile of the appraiser you are interviewing. Our appraiser can give you affirmative, honest answers to these questions. Your jewelry is special to you, and your appraiser should provide you with the special treatment that you and your jewelry deserve.

§§§§§

These questions and answers, and others like them, can be incorporated into your company's training manual if you have one, and can be the basis for role-playing as well. Develop the questions to suit your customer base and those whom you would like to have as customers. Tailor them to the environment you promote in your store, and add, delete, or change questions to adapt to the realities of your place of business. The value of this kind of training cannot be overestimated. Employ it and you will see results.

If you are committed to providing appraisal services in your store, and are determined to make this department profitable rather than burdensome, you will succeed. Whatever portion of the fees are retained by your company after paying for your appraiser and promotion, will go straight to your bottom line. Do not bother deducting the cost of goods—there isn't any.

## A Declaration for Independents

Admittedly, this book is geared toward the retail jeweler/appraiser, rather than the independent appraiser who relies on appraising as a primary source of income. But much of the information applies to the independent as well.

Like the retailer, the independent has to attract and then satisfy clients. Repeat business is not as forthcoming for the independent as it is for the retail merchant. So the independent appraiser has to generate a great deal of ongoing new business. Because most independents operate out of offices or their homes, they do not have the jeweler's storefront to attract walk-in traffic.

The appraisal product is not an impulse item. People rarely decide on a whim, to have jewelry appraised. When they do, it is generally in the store environment where an astute sales associate recognizes the potential need for an appraisal, and sells the idea to the consumer. So the situation of the independent is quite different from that of the jeweler who is trying to build an appraisal department. For the independent, appraisals are the core of the business, rather than a service that is developed to attract more important sales.

The retailer's need to provide the service can prove to be a blessing to the independent appraiser. Many jewelers will never take the time to become professional appraisers—but a certain number of them will go the extra mile to connect with a reliable, professional independent appraiser. With several stores as clients, some independent appraisers make a very good living. They work hard for their income, but their time is still flexible when compared to the "have to be in the store" lifestyle of retailers.

If you find yourself entering into independent contractor arrangements with stores, you may have a unique advantage over many other appraisers. Make it part of your agreement that you have access to the sales records of the stores you do appraisal work for. *This is confidential information, and should not be shared with anyone.* But imagine the pool of data—actual comparable sales—that would be available to you. This makes your appraisals more accurate and realistic, thereby creating even more demand for your services.

Throughout these pages there are ideas and suggestions for marketing, organization, and producing professional insurance appraisal documents. If you aspire to independent appraiser status, most of these ideas are adaptable. In fact, your knowledge and understanding of the retailer's needs might very well prove to be your ticket to a successful independent appraisal business.

# 13

*Uh-Oh, This One is Different!*

## Unusual Scenarios and How to Handle Them

# Is "similar" good enough?

Several years ago I attended an informal talk presented by Cos Altobelli, for more than twenty years chairman of the American Gem Society's Appraisal Committee. I extracted one particular bit of information that has continued to be useful. Altobelli suggested that the following question be asked at the inception of any insurance appraisal. "In the event of a loss, is there any item among these that you would want duplicated identically?" Inevitably, when this question is asked the customer replies, "Gosh, I never thought about that."

We provide the ultimate service to our customers when we put such suggestions before them. Perhaps there is an item, seemingly ordinary to you, that was designed and made for the customer on a special occasion. Maybe the item was a standard production piece at the time it was acquired, but has tremendous sentimental value. Duplicating the item after a loss does not bring it back, but for a sentimental piece, the identical design is certainly more a comfort than something similar or completely different. Your customer might simply thank you for asking, stating that replacement with similar items would be acceptable in all cases. The question will be appreciated; it never hurts to ask.

What we have to understand and impart to our customers in this case is that the cost of duplicating an item is greater than the cost of simply replacing it with one of "like kind and quality." The stated value or replacement cost will be higher, thereby increasing premiums. Most of the time, however, if your customer would want to duplicate an item in the event of a loss, the added premiums are not objectionable. After affirmation of this kind of valuation from the customer, is important to employ proper appraisal methodology.

Duplication of an item will require specific detail, perhaps even more than would be required otherwise. Photograph the piece from as many angles as you deem necessary, and include a ruler in each photo in order to insure that dimensions and proportions are correct. Measure as many dimensions as possible, and state all of them clearly in the descriptive portion of the appraisal. Pay special attention to finish, cut of gemstones, and other details that will contribute to duplication as closely as possible to the original. If there is ever a loss of this item, you will be that customer's hero, both for asking the question originally, and for the quality of your appraisal. You can be sure that most of your appraisal competitors would not have been as informed as you were, and your customer will have a sense of your excellence.

## Irreplaceable or one-of-a-kind items

Imagine that you are faced with the following challenge. You are presented with a mid-19th century Etruscan Revival style bracelet, complete with granulation and cannetille wire work embellishment. The bracelet contains a maker's mark, consisting of an upper case L and C, centered by an Ace of Hearts, all within a horizontal lozenge. Other marks such as the French quality stamp of the time are apparent and clearly visible. Your research, including some written resources partially authored by archivists and historians from Cartier, leads you to believe with some certainty that the maker's mark is that of Louis-Francois Cartier, the first member of that family to engage in jewelry making as part of Cartier's business. If this sounds like a challenging assignment, read on. It gets better.

You submit the bracelet to Cartier for authentication. After waiting several months, and after the bracelet has been examined by several archivists and authenticators with the company, you receive a letter proclaiming that the bracelet cannot be positively authenticated. You are told that the maker's mark has never been seen with a rectangle around the heart. Yet your references repeatedly describe the lozenge-shaped mark as containing the "Ace of Hearts," which more than implies a rectangular shape within the lozenge.

So, not only are you faced with a unique piece of some historical significance in our industry, but you cannot get the authority to authenticate it in writing. How do you proceed with the insurance appraisal? Carefully, of course.

At some point you will have to make a decision. Your customer desires insurance on this most unusual piece. Even as a generic bracelet of the period, it is of very fine quality, in a style that is very popular among collectors, and in beautiful condition. As a product of the early days of the Cartier empire, it has a mystique all its own. This mystique, if authentic, enhances value (or increases replacement cost if you will) in the marketplace. What decision do you make?

Either way, your appraisal should explain very clearly how and why the you reached your decision. In addition, it should state that the stated replacement value is based upon the critical assumption that your authentication, or lack thereof, is correct. You must go on to state that if the assumption is later proven incorrect, the value conclusion would be different. This way, anyone relying on the appraisal will understand the limitations under which you are preparing and signing it.

Your research on value should of course be conducted according to your authenticity conclusion, however tentative. If the piece is simply a generic example of the revival styles of the mid-Victorian period, research should focus on such items. In the highly specialized market for famous maker pieces, your research will be more difficult and time consuming. Such an assignment justifies whatever fee you feel you must charge to do the job correctly. Just be sure to quote at least a range of what you expect to charge, in advance of beginning this lengthy assignment, and preferably in writing.

## How about famous makers like Cartier, Tiffany & Company, Van Cleef & Arpels, and others?

Authentication issues can arise with contemporary jewelry also. Signatures are sometimes imitated. Famous jewelry houses may not provide price information on an item unless they can examine it for authenticity. Some will refuse to provide information because they prefer to perform the appraisal in their own offices. By developing trusting relationships with these companies, you may be able to derive some or all of the information you require when their items come to you for appraisal.

Sometimes those relationships simply cannot be developed, because company policy prohibits the dispensing of information to appraisers. Angry, accusatory talk does not eliminate the barriers (though some have tried this technique in the past). It is best to develop a working knowledge of how each company functions, then operate as well as possible within that context. You might have to learn to "shop" these exclusive stores in order to obtain the information you require. One appraiser routinely faxes photographs of jewelry items to famous makers, under the guise of attempting to purchase a similar piece for his wife.

This is not to encourage devious behavior. The greatest appraisal good is served when retailers cooperate with professional appraisers. When the cooperation is not forthcoming, the professional appraiser becomes a detective and conducts research as necessary always taking care to avoid creating a negative impact.

## What about components that might be damaged?

On the surface this next discussion might appear to deal with rather obscure issues.  But it is worth thinking about, and you will find that the principles applicable here will be useful for other, more commonly occurring assignments.

You receive a call from an insurance company asking you to handle a claim involving a broken opal, which is set in a diamond pendant.  When you meet with the policy holders, you are presented with a 4.25 carat, irregularly shaped (free form pear shape) opal that has split across the center into two pieces.

You are being asked to replace a fine quality, odd-shaped opal measuring 17 mm long, very shallow and flat, with one that matches as closely as possible.  Any replacement will of course have to be approved by the insured.  The replacement opal will have to be the specific shape and thickness of the original, in order to fit into the pendant.  The total insurance coverage for the entire pendant is $3,900.00.

Anyone who has ever tried to match a fine opal knows how difficult that can be.  The nature of opal is such that no two stones are exactly alike, and except for pairs that are matched at the original production stage, matching is extremely difficult.  Generally we have to be concerned with quality and effect, rather than actually trying to match every element of the stone.  So you suggest this philosophy and the policy holders agree.

You send the broken opal to a dealer with whom you have a solid working relationship.  He promises to match the stone during his upcoming trip to Australia, and have the stone cut to size and shape.  One month later you receive the replacement opal.  It is a reasonable match, but your clients reject it.  Fortunately the dealer had promised in advance to take the stone back if it was unacceptable.  But he is also unwilling to pursue the search, because it might result in further loss.

You move on to another supplier, with the understanding that larger pieces of opal will be sent for approval, then the piece that is chosen will be re-cut to fit.  This is where the appraisal issues kick in.  This is not a criticism of the original appraisal, because that was written for the entire pendant as a whole item.  It was prepared by the jeweler who sold the pendant originally, and the $3,900.00 figure was the actual selling price.  Sounds good so far.  But this replacement scenario illustrates an obscure but critical omission from the appraisal.

When items with unusual components (such as this opal, or Old Mine Cut diamonds) are submitted for appraisal, we have to think even more carefully about how that item, or in this case, a component of the item, would be replaced.  Let's say that in the instance we have been dealing with, you finally locate a near-perfect match—a 10.75 carat opal that can be cut to the correct size and shape for the pendant.  Your cost is $350.00 per carat including cutting costs, or nearly $3,800.00 *wholesale* for the finished opal.  This means that the clients are underinsured at $3,900.00, which was the recent purchase price for the entire pendant.  You will have to ask the clients to pay the additional dollars over the covered amount, not to mention convincing an insurance adjuster that you need the entire limit of the coverage, just for the opal.

Could the original appraiser have anticipated this problem?  Could have, yes.  But should have?  Perhaps, but the potential for this replacement scenario is not particularly obvious.

By contrast, a diamond engagement ring with a modern brilliant center diamond and two baguettes would not require this kind of consideration.  There will usually be adequate insurance coverage to replace any one component that may be lost or damaged.  And we know that our client will not have to custom cut any diamond from that ring if replacement is required.  Let's now return to the scenario of the unique opal and see what to do.

After the monetary logistics are worked out and the opal is replaced, how can the new appraisal be handled?  Let us assume that opals of the nature, quality and size of the one that was replaced, are readily available in the retail marketplace at $700.00 per carat.  Multiplied by the 4.25 carat finished weight, that amounts to $2,975.00 retail.  Yet your cost to duplicate (as closely as possible) that opal by purchasing a larger stone and having it cut down, was $3,800.00 at the wholesale level. There is a deficit of $825.00 before any markup.

In the appraisal, you would have to explain clearly, the replacement scenario just discussed. Replacement of the entire pendant with a comparable item (in the event the original item is entirely lost or destroyed) is one angle to pursue. Duplication of the pendant identically, or nearly so, is another approach. And of course the issue of replacing just the opal, to cover a repeat of the process just completed, should be addressed. Even with a conservative 50% markup, the opal alone retails for $5,700.00.

In this assignment you have the advantage of just having completed the replacement scenario, including dealing with the original inadequate insurance coverage. You have also experienced a procedure which is critical to understand in most if not all appraisal situations. The question to ask about every appraisal is, "How will this item be replaced?" More specifically, as in this case, when any component of an item is an issue by itself, it may not suffice to look at the piece as a whole. A separate statement about a particular element will be helpful at the least, and sometimes absolutely necessary. "In the event of a loss, is there any item among these that you would want duplicated identically?" should be a standard pre-appraisal question. A discussion about unusual components is critical as well.

Explain these unusual possibilities in the appraisal, and present more than one value conclusion when necessary. The insurance company and the insured—your client—will be entering into a contract. Give them as much information as you can, to enable them to make the most informed decision possible.

## *"Mine is finer, it's an Old Miner ..."*

The discussion about how to appraise Old Mine and Old European Cut diamonds has been going on for several years. To keep the discussion simple, we will deal with a single diamond ring, with an Old Mine Cut diamond, average diameter of 6.5 mm, bead set in the top of a filigree mounting. Of course your appraisal methodology should begin, as always, with the pre-appraisal interview. "If this diamond is ever lost, would you want to replace it with another Old Mine Cut, or would a modern equivalent be satisfactory?" would be a good question to ask.

If the modern equivalent is the choice made, it is likely that the insurance policy will have to be specifically endorsed for such a replacement. The modern diamond technically does not constitute "like kind and quality," and that might make it an exceptional situation for an insurer. The insurance company's obligation is to replace the item with one of equal *value*. Because antique cut diamonds generally sell for less (all things being equal regarding weight, color, and clarity) than modern equivalents, the modern replacement would have to give up something. For example, if a 1.50 carat Old Mine Cut diamond was lost, a modern diamond of the same weight might have to be a grade or two or more lower in color and clarity, in order for the coverage amount to be adequate. This discussion is somewhat arbitrary without specific diamonds to compare, but it illustrates the point.

Consider the issues. If the diamond falls out of the setting and is lost, a diamond that fits into the setting will have to be found. It might be replaced in a number of ways.

*1.* Find an Old Mine Cut diamond of the correct proportions, of similar weight, color, clarity, and cut quality.

*2.* Find a modern brilliant of the proper dimensions to fit into the setting, also of similar color and clarity, but with obvious differences in cutting style, and probably weight.

*3.* Find a larger modern brilliant or rough diamond, and have it re-cut in the Old Mine Cut style, to the same proportions as the original.

Of the three choices, Number 3 is probably the most expensive, Number 2 next, and Number 1, if achievable, the least expensive. So the most authentic replacement would probably be the least expensive. It is also the least likely to be achieved. So your client has to make a decision, but if he or she cannot, you can include all three scenarios in the appraisal. And as stated before, it might not be the client's decision alone. In these situations, advise your client in conversation and in writing in the appraisal that these matters should be carefully discussed and understood with the insurance company.

The insurer (and the issued policy) will assume replacement with "like kind and quality" if you do not suggest otherwise. If you appraise the piece as a whole item, containing an Old Mine Cut diamond, you may be short-changing your client in the event of a loss. It could be that the inconvenience of searching for an item of like kind is unacceptable to the client. That is why these options should be explained carefully prior to beginning the assignment. Whatever methodology is used, whichever option(s) you choose, a detailed explanation of your thinking should be included in the descriptive portion of the appraisal report.

For many years the GIA and others independently taught appraisers that the way to appraise antique-cut diamonds was to estimate their re-cut weight (to modern proportions), and use that fictitious new diamond as the basis of value. That methodology is erroneous, given the more logical discussion above. Imagine an Old Mine Cut diamond with a diameter ranging from 5.80 to 7.00 mm. The "re-cut" diameter will be no larger than 5.80 mm. Yet this "new" diamond will have to somehow fill a setting that was occupied by a diamond with a maximum diameter of 7.00 mm. It is likely to fall through the setting, unless the metal (and thus the antique design) are reworked. As appraisers, we do not have the liberty to arbitrarily change an item into something it is not, simply to make our professional lives easier. Any such conversion, if acceptable at all, must be discussed with our clients, and carefully explained in the appraisal report.

If you explain your methodology carefully and the risk is underwritten based upon your appraisal, your customer will have an easier time if a loss occurs. You are also less likely to have an appraisal come back to haunt you.

### *"This item is no longer available." What about old watches?*

Watches are an item commonly submitted for appraisal. The subject of appraising watches is particularly interesting, because watches are machines and therefore subject to deterioration unlike that encountered in other kinds of jewelry. In some cases, the usual "replacement cost new" approach may not apply.

A brand new watch that is currently available model presents a straightforward situation. The watch is brand new, and if it is lost tomorrow it will be easily replaced with a brand new one. The used watch presents a new set of issues.

A customer brings you a fifteen-year-old Rolex wristwatch to be appraised for insurance. Although most insurance companies in actual practice will replace "new for used" (for example, a stolen television set will not have to be replaced with a used one, but rather the nearest equivalent currently available), we cannot be certain that this will always be the case. In fact many if not most policies contain a clause such as "...we will pay...the full amount of our cost to replace the item with one substantially identical to the item lost or damaged."

**A Bug In The Works**

An elderly watch repairman in a West Coast retail store loved to tease and joke with customers. One day he was asked to examine the insides of an old pocket watch that had stopped running. He opened it carefully, examined the movement closely, and declared, "I know what the problem is. The engineer died!" as he gently pulled out a spider that had crawled into the watch and met its end.

This tells us that the insurer may want to replace the fifteen-year-old Rolex with another of similar age and condition. In actual practice this rarely occurs. But we want to protect our customer by providing as much pertinent information as possible. So for a watch that has a new counterpart that is identical or nearly identical to the watch being appraised, provide both values. In this case, let us say our research reveals that a similar used Rolex typically sells for $5,000.00 in the "previously owned" retail market. That should be stated in the appraisal. You may also then present the current replacement price for the "nearest equivalent model" currently available through authorized Rolex agents. It now becomes the job of the policy holder (your customer) and the insurance company to negotiate the terms of coverage. You have provided the information required to make the decision.

Why go to the trouble to research both the new and used markets? If the watch in question currently sells for $14,000.00 new and we only use that figure, our customer may have a rude awakening when the used watch is lost and the insurance company decides to replace it with another used one. Imagine that the policy holder decides to "cash out" instead of having the watch replaced. The settlement offer of $5,000.00 or less will be very disappointing, and there may be repercussions for you because your client paid premiums on $14,000 of value based not on their decision, but upon your appraisal. By following the methodology described above, you build a safety net for yourself, by allowing the two contracting parties (your customer and their insurance company) to negotiate their own agreement regarding coverage.

How about a ladies' wristwatch from the 1970s, 14 karat gold, with no current equivalent model being manufactured by that company? The watch is rather generic in nature despite having the name of a known maker on it. Not only is nothing that looks similar available, but this particular manufacturer no longer produces watches in solid gold. How would you proceed?

Initially you might simplify the process by asking your customer, "Do you have any sentimental attachment to this particular vintage? Would you want to replace it with a similar piece, of similar style and age? Would you prefer that I investigate what other manufacturers have available in a similar style?" Once these questions are answered, you will have a clearer picture of how to proceed. You might indicate replacement value/cost for the watch as-is, with a similar 1970's wristwatch available in the secondhand market. You can also add, if this is the case, that another manufacturer makes a similar watch in 14 karat gold, but with a quartz movement rather than the mechanical movement contained in the watch being appraised. A comment about the difficulty that might be encountered in locating a similar vintage watch, can also be included in the appraisal. This being made clear, the insurance company might choose at the outset to cover the watch for replacement with a new equivalent.

The important point here is that we cannot automatically depreciate the value of a used watch. The insurance company may not do so, and we should not arbitrarily make this decision for them.

Collectible vintage watches such as the Gruen Curvex, vintage Rolex, Hamilton Ventura electric from the 1950's, and others, have a bona fide, trackable second hand market. It is our responsibility as appraisers to understand and, when necessary, research that market when we encounter an appropriate watch of this category for appraisal. Just as you would not appraise a platinum and diamond Edwardian necklace based upon the prices charged for reproductions, you must treat vintage, collectible watches as what they are.

Lastly, keep aware of the marketplace activity for new watches. Certain models, because of extraordinary provenance or publicity, not only are not discounted but bring premiums above and beyond their suggested retail prices. Although this is rare, when it is the case it should be reported and explained in the appraisal, with the appropriate replacement value conclusion consistent with the market reality.

******************

As with all other appraisal scenarios, in unique appraisal situations we have to think about what the assignment has to accomplish and how we want to reach that goal.  Then we have to let the user of the report know what we have done—in writing.

# 14

*Nobody Cares About Appraising*

## Generating Support for Professional Appraisal Practices

Although the jewelry industry as a whole has become more receptive to professional appraisal practices in recent years, there is still resistance to the expenditures of money and energy required to elevate this part of the jeweler's business. In some cases the appraiser is an employee trying to get management to respond to requests for money and support for the appraisal department, and encountering the "there's no money in appraising" attitude. The appraiser may be a partner whose other half is not interested in devoting resources to appraising, with the same rationale. And in some cases the company accepts the importance of appraising, but employees are not excited because there doesn't seem to be any money (i.e., commissions) in it for them. Perhaps this chapter will enlighten appraisers and resisters alike.

## *The employee-appraiser's plight*

Resistance and its breakdown seem to flow in stages, obviously with the strongest resistance encountered early in the appraiser-employer relationship. The resistant employer may not have had the opportunity to see how valuable appraisal services can be in the retail environment. Typical early attitudes, or **Stage 1**:

- We've always done it this way, and we've never had any problems.
- Nobody cares about appraisals.
- Insurance companies will accept anything, so why bother?
- There is no money in appraising; it is a necessary evil.
- It is too easy to get into trouble, so we only appraise what we sell.
- I cannot afford to have a full time appraiser on staff; so you have to be on the sales floor as well.
- You can sell ten thousand dollars in jewelry in the time it take you to do a three hundred dollar appraisal.

After some initial successes, you might find your employer entering **Stage 2**, what I call the "cautious acceptance" stage (also known as, "Okay, so the boss complains sometimes...but at least he is noticing"). This is typified by:

- Hey, we could use a few more big fees like that!
- Hmmm ... Nice job.
- Too bad you can't be this busy *all* the time.
- Can we find a way to save money on the photography?
- The costs are adding up (of course so are the fees in commensurate fashion).
- Start thinking about some ways we can train our other employees to sell appraisal services.
- You spend a lot of time doing clerical work—can we simplify the process?

In **Stage 3**, there are glimmers of acceptance. The employer is beginning to see signs of life in the appraisal department. These may be in the form of add-on retail sales, large fees, attention from attorneys, or other benefits of having a professional appraisal department.

- Have you thought about advertising this service? It is something we should consider.
- Have you started developing training materials for the staff yet?
- Would printed brochures help to grow this business?

- Now that we're seeing some success here, how do you think the appraisals should look cosmetically?
- Do we need new forms? Do we need forms at all?

**Stage 4** marks acceptance and active support, and sees the following attitudes develop in the employer:

- I'd like you to write up some sample advertising for our appraisal services.
- Would a computer help you to produce appraisals faster?
- Is there software that would cut out some of this clerical work? (Yes, there is always *something* to complain about!)
- The brochure dispenser on the front counter needs to be filled again.
- I think we should start setting quotas for the sales staff. Why don't we establish a minimum number of appraisal appointments they have to schedule each month?
- Wow! I never knew what an appraisal *was* until *you* got here.
- Do you see us generating so much appraisal business that we have to hire an assistant for you?

## *Generating support: What the employee-appraiser can do*

I have often heard the newly-educated, zealous appraiser ask, "But how can I get my boss to accept this information and let me run with it? He thinks appraisals are unimportant." The solution to a gradual developing of confidence and support from the employer can also be defined and mapped in stages. During Stage 1, the following will be helpful.

- Try not to incur new expenses until you have demonstrated the value of appraising.
- Use existing forms if they do not compromise your standards and/or ethics.
- Produce the most professional product you can under the circumstances.
- Do as much of the work as you can, including word processing (even if you have to buy an inexpensive computer with your own funds).
- Demonstrate the value of the superior product to fellow employees and your superiors.
    - Show off your professional looking appraisal reports.
    - Tell them about favorable calls or letters from customers.
    - Point out problems with other appraisals that come across your desk.
    - Ask a client who is impressed with your work to write to your employer about their positive experience.
- Work to increase business.
    - Train staff to sell your services.
    - Personally handle as many telephone inquiries as you can.
    - Support other staff in their work in order to encourage them to support your efforts to build an appraisal department.
    - Suggest a sales incentive program to reward associates who are actively supporting your efforts.
- Track retail sales that arise out of appraisal services.
- Demonstrate the value of the superior product to fellow employees and your superiors.
- Consider raising fees if they are not commensurate with your ability and the quality of your work.
- Continuously monitor gross appraisal income compared to the previous year's figures.

If you are the employer/appraiser and find inspiring your staff difficult, try some of the following:

- Stress the importance of the enhanced image that professional appraising brings to your business.
- Create new forms and/or format, take-in forms, and other materials such as brochures.
- Prepare an appraisal business plan and/or appraisal sales goals.
- Conduct training sessions for the following:
  - *w*Take-in procedures.
  - *w*Handling telephone appraisal inquiries.
  - *w*Selling your professional services.
  - *w*Justifying fees to customers.
  - *w*Maximizing the appraisal customer by seizing selling opportunities.
- Track retail sales that arise out of appraisal services and point them out at sales meetings, emphasizing the commission opportunities for alert sales associates.
- Consider raising fees if they are not commensurate with your ability and the quality of your work compared to the competition, taking into account the time expended in producing this professional product.
- Continuously monitor gross appraisal income compared to the previous year's figures, and point out that increased appraisal sales generate increased sales in general.
- Begin making formal presentations of appraisal sales figures, highlighting increases and discussing and reinforcing those methods that have resulted in those increases.
- Continue the things you have been doing that have worked, and you will find that your employees will begin to accept the importance of appraisals to them.

Once the acceptance level is up, you can become more aggressive with training and goals. Consider taking training to the next level. Try role-playing, with you as the customer. Challenge staff to answer your difficult questions and sell the appraisal product. Address typical questions you have heard from customers, such as:

- "That sounds like a lot of money—I think I'll shop around."
- "Can't you complete the appraisal while I wait?"
- "Why do I need all of that detail?"
- "Can you leave out the photographs and charge me less?"
- "I just want to know how much it's worth. Do I really need an appraisal?"

If you haven't already done so by this stage, change over to a format that is most compatible with your standards, ethics, and education. If your brochures and other direct promotional materials are not complete, now is the time. They will help you to accelerate growth in the department.

We are all motivated at least in some degree by the "what's in it for me" mentality. Developing an appraisal department that is profitable and important to your business takes teamwork. The appraiser cannot do everything, but *can* be a leader in selling, marketing, and demonstrating the importance of this service to a retail business. By paying attention to your progress and taking steps to continue it, you may suddenly find yourself with more appraisal work than you can handle. And as my mom would say, "That should be the biggest problem you ever have."

# 15

*The Truth is Out There Somewhere...*

## A Few Words About
## Non-Insurance Appraising

Who's right anyway?

T his is a book about insurance appraising only, so the information in this chapter will be quite limited. It is more a comment on other appraisal functions, than actually meant to educate about them.

Appraisals may be requested for a variety of reasons. They can be required in divorce cases, for submission with a federal or state estate tax return, for charitable contributions, for equitable distribution (to beneficiaries of an estate, or simply because someone wants to gift their jewelry equally to certain parties), to verify the quality and value represented by the jeweler who sold the item, for litigation in a variety of scenarios, and of course "just for my own knowledge." This list is incomplete, and other situations are bound to come your way.

Whether or not you accept these assignments should be dependent upon whether you are qualified to perform the task. It is just as important to know your limitations as it is to know your strengths. Refer an assignment you are not qualified for to someone who is—or simply turn it down. You do not serve yourself, your business, or your client if you do otherwise.

If you take appraisals seriously and have not carefully considered this issue, it is now time to make a decision. Will you educate yourself to take on virtually any appraisal assignment that comes your way? Will you find a qualified independent appraiser to do some or all of this work for you? Or will you simply discontinue those appraisal services you are not qualified for? As an insurance appraisal specialist and appraiser, I have frequently been called upon to review others appraisers' work. I have spoken to some of them in order to clarify the methodology if any) employed in arriving at a value conclusion. The responses have often been appalling. "Isn't fair market value just half of retail?" one jeweler asked. "I sell my diamonds at 50% over cost, and most of my local competitors have similar margins. But isn't keystone the proper markup for all appraisals?" another queried.

Appraisal problems continue partially because of a lack of understanding in our industry of the importance of this arena. Not wanting to turn down business or disappoint a customer, many perfectly honest jewelers blindly dive into appraisal assignments for which they are not qualified. But these jewelers are not being honest with themselves. They are putting themselves and their customers at risk.

Imagine an appraisal for a ***charitable contribution***. Your customer has owned a gemstone for many years, and has decided to donate it to the GIA in order to take advantage of the tax benefits derived from the donation. Not understanding the methodology required for such an appraisal, you appraise the gem at several times the fair market value that is likely to be defensible. This results in an excess tax deduction and reduced tax liability for your customer, and is ultimately not accepted by the Internal Revenue Service. If the tax return is audited, you are likely to be called to defend your work. If you cannot, your customer may pursue legal recourse against you for creating this problem.

Appraisals for Federal estate tax scenarios are governed largely by IRS regulations and procedures, just as those for charitable contributions are. In this case you may once again be jeopardizing your customer's chances for acceptance of the appraisal. An overstated value results in too much tax being paid, and understatement obviously has the opposite effect. You might cause either effect if you are not properly trained in the preparation of tax-related appraisals. You would not prepare tax returns for a customer without the proper qualifications, and in fact the IRS considers appraisers to be tax practitioners. If you are not qualified to do the work, do not do it.

## Some other common appraisal functions

***Consumer resale.*** It is common for retail consumers to ask jewelers for appraisals when what they really want is for the jeweler to make a cash offer for the jewelry. When this is clear, it is best to either make an offer, or suggest another venue for sale. To discuss value, then make an offer, sets up the jeweler for a conflict of interest that can cause bad feelings. No matter how honest you are, at the very least the perception that you appraised low to buy low can be damaging.

---

### The Story Has A Strange Ring To It

A long-time customer came into my store in Los Angeles in 1986. He wanted to sell a white gold ring, set with diamonds and sapphires, and containing a watch movement beneath a gem-set cover. The piece was badly damaged. The spring hinge was broken, some gemstones were missing, the watch did not run, the crystal was broken, and the dial needed refinishing.

I politely told the customer that I really did not want to invest in the watch because of its poor condition and the additional expense required to totally restore it for sale. He said that he understood that he would not get much for the ring, but wanted me to make an offer anyway. I insisted, stating that my offer would be so low as to be insulting to him.

He became more assertive, and absolutely assured me that he would not be insulted by my offer, and that I should go ahead and tell him how much I would pay. I still refused, stating again that I was embarrassed at how little I was willing to pay, and that I did not want to offend him. He insisted once again, so I gave in and offered three hundred dollars.

"What"!!" he hollered. "Do you know who I am?" Of course I knew who he was, but he yelled his name at me anyway. I tried to remind him that I had been reluctant to make the offer. But as his wife called me a crook and a thief they exited the store, never to return.

---

There are times, however, when a resale appraisal is called for and valuable to the customer. You may encounter rare or expensive items that might be sold in a number of different markets. How about a platinum ring in good condition, containing a two carat old mine cut diamond? This ring might be sold over the counter to a jeweler or pawn broker. Sale directly to a private party is an option. Auction is also viable for such an item, and might even bring the strongest price.

The average consumer is in the dark about how and where to sell valuable jewelry. A resale appraisal can take into account all appropriate markets, stating a range of potential realization in each. This multi-market approach provides valuable information that assists the consumer in making an informed decision about where to liquidate the jewelry. The discussion of each market can include, along with potential dollars realized, the length of time it might take to be paid, along with other factors that might influence the decision about where to sell. The auction, though attractive because of the potentially higher realization, might be out of the question for some sellers because of the waiting time for the sale to occur, and for payment afterwards.

***Possible purchase.*** Frequently you will be asked to appraise an item that was recently purchased from a local competitor. Most often—though not exclusively—these assignments involve engagement rings. There are important things to remember if you choose to take on such appraisals. The obvious consideration is the possibility of angering your local competitor. You must handle these appraisals carefully.

There are two likely areas of contention: One is the quality (and possibly, but less likely, quantity) represented, and the other is actual purchase price. There are ways in which to protect yourself from the wrath of another jeweler, yet still provide this valuable service to your clients. One such practice is stating a range of value or common selling price, rather than committing to a specific dollar figure. In reality, what would be considered fair prices do exist within a range. You want your clients to understand that if you state a value of, for example, $3,000.00 for an item, and they paid $3,300.00 for it, this does not in any way indicate that they were cheated. If they were provided with a point of sale "appraisal" stating a value of $5,000.00 for this item, another problem exists—between seller and consumer, if your appraisal is accurate.

If you disagree with any representation of quality or quantity made by the seller, you should say so in the appraisal. Additionally, you should provide two ranges of value. One should reflect the quality represented by the seller. The other should be based upon your opinion of quality and quantity. If you are incorrect in your quality/quantity assessment, you will at least have provided the range of value for the (presumably correct) seller's representation. This makes clear the fact that you have acted with integrity, and without intending to do harm to the seller. Your AID should spell out the purpose and assigned use for the appraisal, along with the methodology and reasoning employed, very carefully. One appraiser suggests calling this kind of an appraisal, "appraisal for purchase." This is usually accurate, as most of these appraisals will be requested within the "no questions asked refund" period allowed by the seller. The appraisal serves as a guide for the consumer, to be used in making the purchasing decision. A note of caution: If you cannot be objective about your competitor's merchandise say so and turn down the assignment, and be truthful about the conflict that prevents you from performing professionally. Your clients and your competitors will appreciate your candor.

**Divorce.** This is a tricky arena, partly because the rules change from one jurisdiction (generally, state) to another. Some states require that property be appraised at fair market value. This might be defined by the state, but some states defer to Federal definition(s). Appraisals for divorce are not for the uneducated. What the attorney wants or needs for the client is not necessarily what is called for by proper appraisal methodology. Before delving into this area, be sure you understand the mechanics of both the law and the appropriate appraisal procedures.

**Conservatorship.** Sometimes the court will assign a conservator to manage the affairs of someone who has become unable to do so because of poor health, old age, or incompetence of some other sort. The court will usually order an appraisal of all of the individual's possessions. The appraised value guides the court and appropriate social agencies in determining the amount of assistance that can be made available. Conservators hire appraisers to provide them with this information. Again, this kind of work is not for the uneducated. You have to be versed in the specific statutes and guidelines that apply to conservatorship in your state. Fair market value is a common requirement, but again, definitions vary and fair market value might not even apply in your state.

**Equitable distribution.** These appraisals will be requested for a number of reasons. The beneficiaries of an estate might ask for such an appraisal, in order to effectively and fairly distribute a decedent's property. An individual sometimes wants to have this appraisal in hand before their demise, in order to save the heirs the trouble of doing so later. There are occasions when your client simply wants to distribute property in the present, and wants to do so fairly. Consistency is critical here. Apply the same value level (i.e., fair market value, retail, etc.) to all items so that they are valued with consistency.

One particular assignment, a variation on equitable distribution, was initiated by a bank trust officer. The survivors of a recently deceased woman were bickering over two pieces of jewelry. Two appraisals had been provided for Federal estate tax purposes. One stated a fair market value of $11,000.00, and the other, $42,000.00! Those beneficiaries who wanted to buy the jewelry, of course wanted the lower value to be binding. The other family members were pushing for the higher value, since the proceeds of the purchase were to go into the estate "pot." So a third appraiser was hired to settle the issue with yet another assessment of fair market value. Having no desire to become part of the already existing battle, this appraiser astutely inquired about the trust officer's next step if the matter could not be settled. The response? The jewelry would be sold through a major New York auction house if that were the case.

The appraiser suggested that the appraisal be written based upon ranges of expected realization for each of the two items in that particular auction venue. He noted that the beneficiaries who wished to purchase the jewelry could start bidding at the lower end of the range stated for each item in the appraisal. The trust officer could reserve the right to consign the jewelry to the auction house, if the potential buyers failed to bid the lowest figure. Grateful for this simple solution, the trust officer hired the appraiser. Ultimately the methodology worked, all beneficiaries agreed to the terms, and the matter was settled quickly.

**Collateral.** This kind of an appraisal is no longer common, as many lenders have become understandably skittish about loaning money secured by jewelry. This is largely because of faulty appraisals, based upon retail values, that resulted in banks being damaged when liquidation became necessary. Occasionally a private individual will approach you with jewelry that is being offered either as collateral against a loan, or to actually pay off a debt.

In any of these cases, the lender will need to know how much money can be realized from the sale, or liquidation, of the jewelry. Retail has no meaning for the lender, unless he or she is a retail jeweler and can sell the property with a store through which the merchandise can be sold. A lender, either institutional or private, might have to get a loan paid off by selling the collateral merchandise. You must consider the avenues open to that lender, and appraise the jewelry accordingly.

– – – – –

By referring appraisal work for which you are not qualified to someone who is, you will demonstrate that you have your customer's best interests in mind. Contrary to popular thinking, your customer's image of you is damaged much more by a problem causing appraisal than it is by your willingness to admit that you are not qualified, and would be doing them a disservice by pursuing the assignment.

Fair market value is clearly defined by the Federal government, and other jurisdictions, such as particular states, may define it differently. Appraisals calling for fair market value, and other scenarios such as those discussed in this chapter, can be challenging and lucrative. Formal education in appraisal methodology and procedures will begin to prepare you for these and other appraisal assignments, along with insurance appraising of course. But without a thorough understanding of the requirements for the assignment at hand, you are treading on dangerous ground. Education is the only answer, and the decision to qualify yourself—or not—for these assignments, is yours and yours alone.

# 16

*All that is Left, is to do What is Right*

## Ethical Considerations for Insurance Appraisals

*"Of course I'm ethical, I'm a nice guy".*

A s we near the end of this book, and look back at the previous chapters, it is clear that a great deal of what we have to learn about appraising is rooted, simply, in doing the right thing. We have obligations to the customer and to the insurance company, both of whom rely on our appraisals. Because of those obligations, it seems logical to address some ethical concerns. Some of the examples will not be specific to insurance appraisals, but you will find that even if insurance is the only appraisal function you choose to pursue, you will be able to apply the principles involved in these ethical challenges.

Appraisers are regularly confronted with opportunities to serve their own interests while ignoring the interests of those who rely on appraisers to have impeccable ethical standards. Ignoring the interests of others might be as simple as appraising an item for the specific value requested by a customer, in the hopes of encouraging that customer's future business.

We might be asked to take shortcuts in order to reduce fees. Remember the story about the client who requested omission of photographs and detailed descriptions in order to save money on the fee?

Retailer/appraisers are often asked to appraise jewelry purchased from their competitors. Inherent in these assignments is the temptation to disparage the other jeweler's merchandise. Even when this abuse of the appraiser's position is not blatant, it might result in an artificially low estimate of value.

Related to the tendency to disparage other jewelers' prices is the tendency to use our own point of sale "appraisals" (which we now know should *not* be called appraisals) to demonstrate our own bargain prices. By stating a value that is 50% or more higher than the actual selling price, we are implying that we are able to sell the item for that much less than it is worth. This of course is not true. If we sell it for that much less than it is worth, our businesses will not survive. Increasingly, the public is catching on to the absurdity of this practice, and some consumers are developing a justified distrust of jewelers who engage in this kind of deception.

If you cannot be unbiased and objective in an assignment, it is best to turn it down. One appraiser was continually being asked to appraise merchandise that was purchased from a local jeweler who chronically misrepresented diamond quality. The appraiser became increasingly frustrated with the four to five grade difference between his assessments and the jeweler's representations. The temptation to disparage the merchandise and slander the jeweler became too great. He had to exercise extreme care in order to keep his personal feelings from clouding his objectivity.

## Ethics Defined

One dictionary definition of ethics is "the system or code of morals of a particular philosopher, religion, group, profession, etc." Though this chapter is not an attempt to establish a firm code of ethics (I leave that task to appraisal associations), some important aspects of our ethical obligations should be addressed.

It is important not to confuse honesty with ethics. One might be the most honest and upstanding citizen, and still behave unethically. Understanding the ethics of a profession goes beyond basic honesty. It is also important to note that the *appearance* of behaving unethically can be as problematic as the behavior itself. If a customer perceives that your actions are unethical, it may be difficult to prove otherwise.

An example: You are asked to appraise a diamond that your customer wants to sell. You appraise the diamond knowing full well that you would like to make an offer to purchase it.

## Seller beware! (and the appraiser should be careful too)

A couple went into a store asking for prices on a particular quality one carat diamond. They were very specific about color, clarity, and weight, as though they had shopped extensively and were ready to make a decision. A salesperson spent some time working with the customers, who eventually left quite abruptly. Several hours later a woman stopped in with a diamond that fit the precise description of the earlier inquiry. She wanted to have the diamond appraised in order to resell it privately. The salesperson overheard the conversation and alerted the store's appraiser to the visit paid by the couple earlier in the day.

The connection was made between the two, of course, and a conversation ensued with the owner of the diamond. She explained that she had advertised the diamond in the newspaper, and that a couple had expressed interest. They were beginning to negotiate price, and wanted to have the diamond appraised before making an offer. She decided to have it appraised on her own prior to entertaining any offers.

An appointment was made to have the diamond appraised later that same day. Prior to the woman's return with the diamond, the gentleman half of the buying couple called the store and asked to speak to the appraiser. He was upset because the seller had come in to the same store where he had attempted to get information. He felt that now the appraiser was obligated to appraise the diamond in his presence! The appraiser explained that, because the man had entered the store under the guise of wanting to purchase from the store, there was no ethical obligation to him as an appraisal customer. In fact, the appraiser's obligation was to the seller, who had pursued information honestly by requesting an appraisal.

The buyer insisted that the appraiser had to allow him to be present during the appraisal process. The appraiser explained that because the seller was paying the fee, it would be her decision as to who would or would not be present while the diamond was examined. Still undaunted, the buyer tried one more ploy. "I know why you don't want me there," he accused. "How do I know you won't raise the grade and the value if she slips you a few extra bucks?" "You don't," the appraiser replied, "but I pride myself on my high ethical standards. I do not do business that way, and regardless, I am not answerable to you. I would suggest that you hire your own appraiser to examine and evaluate the diamond. Then the two of you can negotiate using the information you have acquired on your own behalf." "But then *I* have to pay for another appraisal," he complained. "What are you trying to hide, anyway?" It was then that the appraiser ended the conversation, insisting firmly but professionally that he would not allow his ethical standards to be compromised by a third party interest in the property. He also insisted that he would have nothing to do with someone who was challenging his integrity when in fact he was protecting his client's interest and his own ethical standards. In this case the ethical decision was clear, but dealing with that customer was a challenge.

You might be thinking, "If I appraise this low, I will have a better chance of buying it low." If you are morally opposed to this scheme and educated in the proper methodology, you can appraise the diamond honestly, writing a multi-market appraisal that examines several liquidation options such as sale into the trade, private sale through the newspaper, and sale at auction. The second alternative sounds honest enough. But is it ethical? You still have a conflict of interest. You want to buy the diamond, yet your customer is relying on your supposedly unbiased opinion of value in order to make a financial decision.

There are two basic ways to handle this situation. One, you can simply state that you are uncomfortable with the obvious conflict of interest, and that you would prefer to make an offer rather than appraise the diamond. By explaining that you are thereby saving the customer a possibly unnecessary appraisal fee, you might make a friend and purchase the diamond as well. By dealing with the dilemma in this way, rather than issuing what appears to be a definitive statement on the diamond's worth, you are allowing the seller the freedom to shop for other offers.

The other option is to write the appraisal, but indicate clearly in your conversation *and in writing in the appraisal*, that the conflict of interest exists. State clearly that you have informed the client of this conflict, and that you have nevertheless been retained to render the appraisal report. It is not a bad idea to have the client sign a release acknowledging his or her awareness and understanding of this conflict and the decision to proceed with the appraisal anyway.

You might have entered into this assignment with the honest intentions, only to be accused later of abusing your position as a valuation expert. If you are careful to look at issues of honesty and appearances of honesty from your customer's point of view, you will have greater insights into the ethical issues that confront appraisers regularly. To simply write the appraisal without discussing the conflict, would be unethical even if the appraisal was accurate and unbiased. Technically and ethically, the bias exists because of your interest in purchasing the property

It is the opinion of some individual appraisers that we should never appraise an item that we wish to purchase, and that it is always unethical to do so. Certainly one can never be *too* ethical. But whether or not to appraise an item you intend to purchase is a business decision, and as such, under no circumstances should you engage in this dual role without full disclosure of the effect that it might have on your client's best interests being served.

### Contingency Fees

It is surprisingly common for appraisers to charge contingency fees. When it comes to charging a percentage of value, the conflict is obvious and quite serious. As noted in Chapter 1, the practice is ethically unsound. Even the most honest appraiser might be tempted to "go with the higher number," if it means a higher fee. "After all," one might reason, "an extra thousand dollars of value only costs the client fifteen dollars or so a year in insurance premiums ... but it results in an extra *thirty* dollars for me at three percent of value." Again, even if you are above such temptation, the *perception* that you might overstate value to increase your fee can be as damaging as the actual practice of doing so. In short, how much you are paid, or even whether you are paid, should not be contingent upon your value conclusions.

### Disclaimers of Responsibility

Some pre-printed appraisal forms contain wording such as "The appraiser assumes no liability with respect to any action which may be taken on the basis of this appraisal." There are differing opinions about the inclusion of this wording in your appraisals. One attorney advised an appraiser that, although the statement would not hold up against legal scrutiny, it is advisable to keep it in the appraisal. His reasoning: It discourages the legally uninformed client from filing a monetarily minor, nuisance lawsuit.

Ethically, of course, we cannot dismiss ourselves arbitrarily from responsibility for our work. Nor can we do so legally. The courts repeatedly hold appraisers responsible for the effect their work has on consumers. Because there are no licensing requirements for personal property appraisers, the courts are currently the only agency we can rely upon to regulate this activity. Admittedly this regulation occurs after the fact. However, as more cases are heard and publicized, appraisers will naturally be more careful about what they commit to writing.

## *Dispensing Insurance Advice*

It is not uncommon for a customers to ask questions about insurance coverage. They might ask your advice about which items to schedule and which to omit. Recommend that your customers seek this advice from an insurance agent who is licensed and qualified to have the discussion.

It is important for appraisers to be able to discuss insurance intelligently, and dispensing basic information about replacement procedures is not an ethical breach. But we must be careful not to become inadvertent insurance consultants.

It is advisable to familiarize yourself with standard insurance policies that cover valuables such as jewelry. You can then ask your inquiring customer to bring his or her policy in, so that you can point out the section or sections that pertain to jewelry coverage and potential losses. Again, inform the customer that final determinations about the kind of coverage desired and which items to schedule should be decided by the customer after consulting with the insurance agent.

Some jewelers have arbitrarily decided that any item with a retail replacement value less than five hundred dollars need not be scheduled on a jewelry floater. This may or not be true, depending upon the nature and limit of the basic homeowner's coverage for non-scheduled valuables, and the number of such lower value items the customer owns. You certainly would not give this advice to someone who owns forty items valued at an average of three hundred dollars ($12,000.00 total), but only carries $1,000.00 of basic coverage with a five hundred dollar deductible. Explain the issues that your customer will want to confront in making the decision, but do not advise as to what that decision should be. Once again, leave this kind of advice to the insurance agents. They earn a living by providing it.

## *The Client's Influence*

Your customer might have a motive for a higher or lower than realistic value to be stated in an appraisal. We have to resist such requests, despite our desire to please the customer. The consequences of acceding to your customer's wishes might seem insignificant. It is not uncommon for appraisers to be asked to keep values low, in order to limit premiums. This might seem harmless enough. In fact, some jewelers assume that the insurance company makes too much money anyway, and this is a way to fix the problem.

Not only is it not our place to make such decisions, it is simply unethical to manipulate value. It is also dangerous. Imagine the customer who pressured you to keep values low if a loss occurs and the customer finds himself underinsured. Will that customer remember his request, or will selective memory take over? You run the risk of being sued when your customer's insurance coverage is not sufficient to cover a loss. The mere thought of such a lawsuit should be motivation enough to behave ethically.

An attorney might urge an appraiser to artificially reach a specific value conclusion. We must remember at all times that appraisers are not advocates. We do not manipulate facts in order to argue our customer's case. Attorneys' arguments on behalf of their clients are based upon the facts. Therefore, it is facts that we must provide. I once informed an attorney who was requesting high values that would benefit his client, that I did not engage in such unethical practices. The attorney, in turn, informed me that I would not be hired for this appraisal assignment. In a conversation about proper appraisal methodology in divorce cases, one attorney noted, somewhat tongue in cheek, that "I wouldn't call *you* if I wanted an appraisal for my divorce client. I'd call someone who would give me what I *want!*" Despite the occasional temptations to do otherwise, appraisers have to present the facts in an objective, unbiased manner.

### Oral Appraisals: Dangerous Territory

Jewelers are asked frequently, "How much is this worth?" A good response to this question is usually another question: "Why do you need to know this item's value?" Unfortunately, "I just want to know for myself" is often the response. In these situations, you must continue to question the customer. Is this for insurance purposes? If so, the customer will need an appraisal and you have an opportunity to sell the service. Does the customer want to sell the item? Many times the first question is really a request for an offer to purchase. There are many other reasons for wanting to know what something is worth. As an appraiser, or even as a jeweler who does not appraise, you need to find out why the request is being made.

Value issues are important, and they should be dealt with professionally and in writing. If you transmit value information orally, there is always a possibility that it will be relayed inaccurately, and someone will be damaged or believe they were damaged. The ethical dilemma is clear. Limit value statements to those you can put in writing, in a professionally prepared appraisal document. This eliminates your reliance upon your customer to accurately recall and relate your opinion of value.

"Appraisal Days," often promoted by antique malls and other organizations as public relations events, can be dangerous in the same way. At one such event, an appraiser innocently rendered an oral opinion of value on a piece of antique jewelry. He stated a value of "around $2,000.00." His cursory examination, all he could possibly manage under the pressure of people lined up to see him, had failed to reveal important aspects of the piece. In fact, the item was being offered at $5,000.00 by another dealer in the same antique mall! The customer had asked to have it looked at and evaluated before making the purchase. The price was fair as it turned out, but the appraiser's hastily composed oral opinion killed the sale, and a lawsuit was narrowly averted. No doubt in other such cases the appraiser might not be so fortunate.

Appraisers have to be aware of the potential ramifications of their actions. Oral opinions of value can be damaging to our customers or to third parties. So consider it unethical to offer such opinions, and restrict your appraisals to those you are willing and able to put in writing.

The term "Heirloom Discovery Day" has been used as a substitute for "Appraisal Day." Not only is this term more romantic, it also effectively removes value issues from the equation. It is more accurate to explain that the purpose of the event is to determine whether an item has merit, then to suggest that the specific value of an item will be quoted. Once it has been determined that an item does have merit, the discussion can turn to whether or not the owner should have an appraisal done in order to accurately and professionally identify, authenticate, and evaluate the item.

### Unfamiliar Items

As your appraisal business grows, the variety of jewelry you are asked to appraise will naturally increase. You are then more likely to see pieces that are out of the realm of your expertise. Most of the time you can overcome your lack of knowledge with proper research. However, you might see an item that is beyond your ability to reasonably research. Antique jewelry is a good example. Some jewelers simply appraise antiques as though they are new (using the cost approach—adding up the value of the components), then add a percentage premium for antique value. This is a dangerous practice, subjecting the customer to potential irrecoverable loss as a result of being underinsured. Such an appraisal and result can easily land an appraiser in court. Consider it unethical to appraise jewelry with which you are not familiar, unless you are willing to engage in thorough and proper research.

There is another aspect of this situation that you should consider. You might be able to appraise that antique piece if you do several hours of research that a more expert appraiser in this area would find unnecessary. Your customer has a right to know if you plan to charge for the extensive research time. Explain that you are capable of doing the research, but that it will probably result in a higher fee than might be paid to someone more familiar with the type of jewelry in question. Sometimes you will get the assignment anyway, and sometimes not. In either case, your customer will appreciate your honesty. The other alternative is to do the research for your own education and not charge for the extra time. Chalk this up to experience, and know that the knowledge you gain will benefit you later.

There might be a need to call in an expert who can authenticate a piece or otherwise conduct research that is out of your area of expertise. If this is the case, be sure that you state clearly that this expert participated, and describe the extent of the participation. It is also advisable to have that expert sign his or her portion of the appraisal.

## Hypothetical Appraisals

There are occasions when you will be asked to appraise jewelry that you have never seen before, and it happens more often than you might think. Appraising in this situation is ethically acceptable if you follow certain procedures. We will restrict this discussion to insurance matters. Typically it involves jewelry that was not scheduled on an insurance floater. On one occasion a client of mine left ten pieces in her athletic club locker, and it was all stolen. Except for two sales slips, she had no documentation at all to verify that she had owned the jewelry. The insurance company asked her to have the stolen items appraised in order to facilitate the claim settlement. She had a $5,000.00 coverage limit because of an upgrade to the basic homeowner's policy, and a small deductible. She came to me with a good question: "How can you appraise the jewelry if you can't examine it?"

Item by item, we listed and described the jewelry from the customer's memory. We walked from one showcase to the next, looking for similar items. In one case, for example, she noted that her rope chain was not quite as thick as the one in the case, and that it was two inches shorter. We were able to interpolate to arrive at the approximate replacement cost for the lighter, shorter chain. The entire appraisal was completed in this manner, and a detailed explanation was made in the report itself. The insurance company paid the limit of the policy and the customer was able to replace most of her jewelry immediately.

There is an important principal at work whenever a hypothetical appraisal is written. The International Society of Appraisers in its Core Courses, has used the term **critical assumption**. We make several such assumptions when we prepare this kind of an appraisal. Wording such as the following should be included prominently in the appraisal. "The estimates of value stated in this appraisal are based upon the critical assumptions that the customer actually owned the items described, and that the descriptions provided are honest and reasonably accurate. Any evidence to the contrary, if introduced into the appraisal process, would be likely to alter the estimates of value, perhaps significantly. No investigation has been made to verify the facts represented by the insured."

A statement such as this alerts the insurance company officially (common sense would dictate most of what is in the statement) that you have relied upon the recall and integrity of their client, and based your conclusions upon the information provided to you.

## Fees and Other Surprises

It is a sound ethical policy to avoid springing surprises on your customers. Always define your fee in advance, even if it must be a range. This way, your customer knows at least what the maximum charge will be.

If you find during the appraisal process that unexpected gemological examination or research are required, you can increase the fee—but not before informing your customer and obtaining permission to proceed.

### *Representing Your Qualifications*

In promoting your appraisal business, take care to represent your qualifications accurately and honestly. As one International Society of Appraisers (ISA) instructor used to say, "You are not entitled to say 'Princeton University 1990' on your resume just because you attended a fraternity party there!"

On a more serious level, however, representations of your qualifications and background should not be exaggerated or misleading. If you attended Princeton University for one year, say so. To simply say "Princeton University" is vague and implies that you earned a degree.

To say "gemologist" if you have not earned such a title through proper education and testing is also misleading if not completely false. If you passed one course at GIA, say so. To say, "Gemological Training, GIA" is not clear enough. It may be true that you received some training, but it is unethical to imply anything more.

In general, appraisal societies have varying membership levels, determined by criteria such as completion of courses, years of experience, and submission of sample appraisal reports. It is unethical to misrepresent your qualifications to use such a designation. ISA, for example, has an associate membership level for those who are involved with appraising but have not taken ISA's courses. Only those who have completed the courses and passed the exams are entitled to use the "ISA" designation after their names. Yet, associates have been known to use the title without regard for the rules. Some simply advertise, "Member, International Society of Appraisers," which is not allowed without having earned the "ISA" designation.

In addition to the ethical considerations inherent in the way you represent your qualifications, there are legal ramifications. Your false claims to qualifications you do not possess might return to haunt you. For example, your credibility in a court of law can be destroyed by one misrepresentation on a resume or professional profile.

### *Conclusion*

During the ethics section of an ISA course offering, one of the students made what seemed to some like a simplistic observation. "If everyone just followed the Golden Rule," he noted, "we wouldn't have any need for this ethics section." And actually, he was right.

In any situation that is ethically challenging, simply put yourself in the place of your customer. Forget about how honest you are for a moment, and imagine how you would perceive your actions if you were in your customer's place, dealing with you. How would you want to be treated? Would you want to work with someone who disclaims responsibility for an appraisal? Would you want the jeweler who will be making an offer on your diamond to be the appraiser as well? Would you want to pay a percentage of your jewelry's value? The answers to these and other such questions will provide obvious responses to ethical dilemmas.

As Kevin Moody points out in his Foreword, it is all very much about how good you want to be. If we set our goals as appraisers with our customers' best interest in mind, we will be on target to be successful in this area. By taking care of your customer's needs, you take care of yourself and your business.

# 17

*To Every Appraisal, Learn, Learn, Learn*
*There is a Reason, Learn, Learn, Learn*

## Education–The Great De-Equalizer

Of the thousands of people writing jewelry appraisals, only a tiny percentage have ever engaged in formal appraisal education. As evidenced by the hundreds, rather than thousands, who are members of appraisal organizations that provide formal education, there is relatively little interest in the subject.

Better said, there is relatively little interest in appraisal excellence. Certainly the subject arouses the interest of many jewelers. Whether they are serious about appraising as a profession or not, jewelers seem ready to vent about appraisals in one direction or another. Some rant and rave about how "appraisal nerds" are making too big a deal about the subject. Others are appalled at the lack of professionalism displayed by the typical appraisal

What is typical, anyway? The most common form of appraisal seems to be the handwritten, perhaps legible, two- or three-line description presented on a standard form (with standard disclaimers of responsibility such as "the appraiser assumes no liability for any action which may be taken on the basis of this appraisal"), often but not always at the point of sale. Disclaimers notwithstanding, appraisers are consistently held legally responsible for the damage done by their work.

A typical item description: "Lady's 14 karat engagement ring with one diamond, 1.01 carat, H-I color, I clarity, beautiful cut, and ten side diamonds, 1/2 carat total." Of course no photographs are included.

As discussed in Chapter 8 on the AID, this lack of documentation is not acceptable. Is the ring white or yellow gold? How are the diamonds set? What are some of the proportion characteristics of the center diamond, and what is the quality of the side diamonds? What does the mounting look like? Is "I" clarity $I_1$, $I_2$, $I_3$? This appraisal is obviously the work of someone who has not thought about the life cycle of the appraisal report. How will it be utilized when a loss occurs?

We cannot assume that every jeweler will instinctively go through that process of projecting into the future. This discussion so far is on the simplest level, but it applies to appraisal issues in general. Jewelers cannot be expected to think of everything. They join groups to learn about things such as inventory and payroll management, computerizing their stores, personnel issues, making a repair department profitable, and just about any other subject that applies to their business. So why the lack of interest in appraising?

In the minds of most people, the subject of appraising is esoteric on a *good* day. It has long been seen as the stomping ground of the intellectuals (or pseudo-intellectuals) who hang out at Tucson bars every February, arguing over whether or not fair market value can be determined in this marketplace or that. One gentleman I spoke to referred to these folks as "the direct descendants of the medieval philosophers who tried to determine how many angels could dance on the head of a pin." Although this was said in jest, to much of the jewelry industry the subject is nearly that obscure.

Worse yet, appraisers for several years were heard arguing over who knew more, what society had the most to offer, whose perceptions of the appraisal profession were right and whose were wrong, and various other personal political issues that the jewelry industry masses do not give a hoot about.

I hate to equate appraising with religion, but in a sense the subject arouses an almost religious fervor among advocates of professional appraisal practices. So the important lesson is that, as appraisal students, we have to extract as much meaningful material as possible, and assimilate it into our practice of appraising. This does not mean that you discard something just because you do not want to bother with it. But if you avail yourself of the education that is available, and the networking and advanced educational opportunities that are attached to it, you will find a level of comfort. You will eventually decide how deeply, or not, you want to get into appraising. You will extract that which is meaningful and decide how to responsibly and ethically deal with the rest.

### *"Appraisal classes are too expensive and time consuming."*

This is the rallying cry of the uninitiated. Yes, appraisal classes are expensive. Residence offerings from various organizations will cost thousands of dollars to complete, after taking into account the cost of travel, lodging, food, and the courses themselves. But the costs are dramatically outweighed by the benefits. I recall my gem identification instructor at the GIA, justifying the "miss one and fail" grading system on the final gem identification exam. "We would rather have you make the mistake here than in your business, where it may *cost* you your business," she said firmly. "So we will not let you out of here until you score 100% on this exam."

As the saying goes (sort of), "One bad appraisal can ruin your whole day." Even if you have been appraising jewelry for years, there will always be things you do not know. There are situations that require creative thinking backed by technical appraisal expertise. The best golfers and tennis players have coaches and teachers. There is always something to learn. As evidenced by the frequency with which wholly inadequate insurance appraisals turn up in our industry, there is plenty to learn!

So the question is not really whether it is too expensive and time consuming to take some appraisal courses, but whether it is too expensive *not* to take appraisal classes.

### *Gain vs. cost*

The potential gains from your appraisal education far outweigh the costs in time or money. Even if you do not become a serious professional appraiser, your ability to have appraisal discussions with clients and colleagues will enhance your ability to do business. If you are in the insurance replacement business, or want to be, a thorough knowledge of the mechanics of appraising is not only valuable, but necessary. Your insight into the problems presented by inadequate appraisals, and your ability to deal with those weaknesses and interpret them with a positive solution for your clients, cannot be measured in dollars alone.

You may have been confronted at some time with an appraisal of merchandise you sold, performed by another jeweler. Perhaps you have experienced the unpleasant challenge of trying to explain that your price was fair, that the appraisal was not fair, and that you were being victimized by the appraisal. A thorough working knowledge of the subject will allow you to concisely and expertly explain the problems with the appraisal, without sounding whiny. You will solidify a relationship you may have previously struggled just to maintain.

### *Recovering the expenses: How long will it take?*

If you make plans to invest several days and two or three thousand dollars in appraisal courses, it is perfectly natural to ask yourself, "When will the return on this investment be forthcoming in cash? When will I recover my expenditures?" As usual the answer is not absolute. But there is an answer.

In one year, within the structure of a retail store, my top three billings for single appraisal assignments were $13,000.00, $4,500.00, and $2,700.00. Two of the three (the highest and lowest) were insurance appraisals. In any retail jewelry store these are meaningful individual sales. It is absolutely assured that none of these three appraisal projects would have been given to me were it not for my education and continuing networking and ongoing striving for excellence. How can you measure what you invest in order to attain the professional level required to obtain such assignments?

Like any professional education, the measure is in your daily use (or non-use) of the knowledge of principles and procedures acquired in your educational efforts. As jewelers we are always concerned with value. We sell value on a daily basis. Why is your diamond ring a better purchase than your competitor's? All other things being equal in the mind of the consumer, you have to sell value: service, customer satisfaction, guarantees of quality, and value-added products, such as insurance documentation provided free of charge, all address the issue of value in a purchase. The best salespeople impart the value of the item being considered. Without going into specific selling techniques, we generally understand that the total package associated with the purchase is often what closes the sale.

What does this have to do with appraising? The preparation of an appraisal that is accepted by both the client and any third party (the insurance company, for example) is an exercise in selling. Your appraisal report has to justify the estimate of value, the dollar figure that users of appraisals are ultimately concerned with. The entire report is a sales presentation. If it is convincing, the dollar figure has more weight.

The proof is in the practice. Most appraisals are not questioned by insurance company underwriters. But the true test is in the amount of referral business that comes directly from both clients and third party recipients. Professional appraisers may be called by underwriters on a regular basis to review appraisals that look less than legitimate. The likelihood of having an appraisal questioned is severely diminished by convincing documentation and explanatory material.

The exercise of justifying a stated estimate of value is itself a sophisticated level of selling. It is selling without deception, simply by laying out the facts and drawing a conclusion. The experience of employing these principles and techniques in a retail sales presentation is enlightening indeed.

## Appraisal societies: To join, or not to join?

If appraising is a serious and valued (no pun intended) part of your business, following up your education with professional networking is imperative in your development. In addition to referrals, which are an obvious outgrowth of knowing people and making them aware of what you do, the ongoing opportunities to grow within the structure of an appraisal society are extensive.

By following and participating in the activities of an appraisal association, you will be naturally inclined to continue learning. You may be asked to participate in the creation of a lecture or seminar. What you will learn from the process of creating such a presentation will far outweigh the information you contribute to your colleagues. The presentations you make will in turn demonstrate to those colleagues that you are a cut above average, and that you are worth knowing. If you are worth knowing, people will share with you, and you will learn even more.

There are also hidden side benefits. One appraiser told me that he finally broke down and learned how to use a sophisticated word processing program simply because he had developed such a busy lecture schedule that he had to be able to make his own overhead transparencies and other visual aids. This was someone who five years prior, had never made a public speech in his life! He was inspired to do his first public speaking because of his newfound interest in appraising and related consumer issues. One thing truly did lead to another.

Any appraisal society that values its membership will schedule conferences. These gatherings focus on continuing and advanced appraisal and product information. Your attendance will enable you to continue your networking activities, and to learn from some of the premier personalities and technicians in the appraisal profession, and jewelry industry in general. Conferences will spark new ideas, and help to keep you informed about new appraisal principles, legal ramifications, and methodologies that have been tried either successfully or not.

One of the major complaints about some appraisal courses was that students were not given enough practical, hands-on information about actually producing appraisal reports. The foundation courses did not include the actual creation of complete appraisal reports. The International Society of Appraisers (ISA) filled a huge gap with the addition of a supplemental one-day report-writing seminar. The seminar was specifically designed to tie up the loose ends that may have existed in courses offered by ISA and other organizations. Everyone I spoke to who attended the seminar said it was the single most valuable day in all of their appraisal education—just because it closed so many of the gaps in their prior education.

Advanced courses are also available through some of the appraisal groups. These can include advanced insurance principles, expert witness testimony, and other subject matter that can be very useful. It is important to mention again that much of what you learn, you may not use in an appraisal assignment—ever. But the knowledge will be useful some time, somewhere, and probably when you do not expect it.

Attending the activities sponsored by your appraisal organization will also send a special message to your customers. By announcing your attendance through press releases, direct mailings, or other media, you will be setting yourself apart from most of your competitors. You may receive an award or certificate of appreciation for a project you have worked on. Display these documents proudly—they say a lot about your ability, desire, and integrity. One appraiser left a greeting on his voice mail stating that he was attending an appraisal conference. When he returned, a customer called and exclaimed, "...four days at an appraisal conference—I'm impressed," and proceeded to make an appointment to have her jewelry appraised.

The power of your involvement with other appraisers on an ongoing basis cannot be ignored. From referrals to increased knowledge and insight, the benefits are astounding. As in all phases of your business, you will only be truly successful if you continually strive to be the best you can be. Your education and association with other professionals will assure that you continue steadily toward that goal.

# Some Final Thoughts About Appraising

Like any aspect of your business that is not fully developed (and some that are), appraising can be challenging and frustrating. It is easy to get discouraged, and many jewelers have simply stopped providing the service or have hired independent contractors to handle their appraisal needs.

In the case of the former, the decision is best reconsidered. Appraisals attract new customers and make existing ones happy. Aside from a handful of independents who are well known in their communities, who do consumers wish to have appraising their jewelry but their trusted retailer? As to hiring independents, this is a viable way of handling the burden, if you see it as such.

The process of learning appraisal techniques can in itself be a burden or a joyous experience, depending upon your orientation and intellectual interests. It can be fascinating and fun. The important thing is that you continue to improve your appraisal product as you would any other product in your store. If one of your manufacturers is not producing the quality you need, you ask for improvement and, if necessary, change suppliers. This book sheds some light on the qualities an insurance appraisal requires to truly serve your customers. If the appraisal product is not doing its job and may cause or be a problem, it has to be improved.

Hopefully, you have a great deal more to think about than you did before you read this book. Because there is a certain amount of subjectivity in this constantly evolving profession, this book does not contain all of the answers. Hopefully it has, at the very least, generated all of the questions. As a result, you will be aware when a question has to be answered before you proceed with an appraisal assignment.

Finally, thank you for buying the book, and for caring enough about appraisals to spend your money on it. I welcome your comments in care of the publisher, and will answer your letters personally. Good luck in your pursuit of appraisal excellence. I hope you will always remember this book as a positive step toward that end.

The following organizations provide appraisal education and programs.

**American Gem Society**
8881 West Sahara Ave. Suite 130
Las Vegas, NV  89117
(702) 255-6500

**American Society of Appraisers**
P.O. Box 17265
Washington, D.C.  22070
(703) 478-1700 or 1-800-ASA-VALU

**Appraisers Association of America, Inc.**
386 Park Avenue South, Suite 2000
New York, NY  10016
(212) 889-5404 or fax (212) 889-5503

**Gemological Institute of America**
1660 Stewart Street
Santa Monica, CA  90404
(310) 829-2991 or 1-800-421-7250

**International Society of Appraisers, Inc.**
16040 Christensen Road, Suite 320
Seattle, WA  98188
(206) 241-0359 or fax (206) 241-0436

**National Association of Jewelry Appraisers**
P.O. Box 6558
Annapolis, MD  21401-0558
(301) 261-8270

# SAMPLE APPRAISAL

# Ralph Joseph Jewelers

91263 Diamond Blvd., Suite 5153
Hometown, New Jersey 08888
(609) 123-4567

# JEWELRY APPRAISAL

**Prepared for**

Dr. and Mrs. Ross Stevens
918 Princeton Avenue
Harvard, New Jersey 08887

May 1, 1996

# Ralph Joseph Jewelers

91263 Diamond Blvd., Suite 5153
Hometown, New Jersey 08888
**(609) 123-4567**

May 1, 1996
Prepared for:

**Dr. and Mrs. Ross Stevens**
**918 Princeton Avenue**
**Harvard, New Jersey  08887**

### Purpose and Assigned Use

This Appraisal Report, covering three (3) jewelry item(s) is prepared for the purpose of estimating the retail replacement value(s) of the item(s) described herein, solely for the assigned use of obtaining or renewing insurance. *Use of this report for resale or other non-insurance purposes is likely to mislead potential buyers or other third parties.*

### Basis of Value

Values stated reflect replacement costs for comparable new items currently available or exact duplicates when indicated, except in the case of antique or period pieces or substantially, noticeably used pieces, in which case stated value is for replacement with a comparable item in similar condition. To be "comparable," a piece need not be an exact duplicate or even nearly a duplicate of the appraised item, but rather must be similar enough in vintage, style, utility, and condition to be able to be compared to it. As employed in this report, the term *retail* is defined as "a purchase made for personal use by the ultimate or final consumer."

The value estimate is based upon current information on the date of appraisal, and no representation is made regarding future or past value or with regard to other types of value, such as a price which may be realized by a private party in selling the item(s). The value(s) stated in this appraisal report are based upon replacement cost in appropriate retail markets, and it is important to note that an insurance company's actual cost of replacement may be lower.

In addition to available market information, consideration is given to design execution, quality, desirability, and period of execution.

Value estimates are derived from the appraiser's knowledge and ongoing market research, which may be supplemented by consulting appropriate specialists and/or through research in auction catalogs and other local and national sources for similar items.

### Sales Tax

Individual estimates of value in the appraisal do not include sales tax. A sales tax total calculated at the current local rate is usually stated with the total estimate of value at the end of the description portion of the appraisal. Due to the fact that Ralph Joseph Jewelers serves clients in more than one state and the sales tax rates vary, sales tax may not be included in every appraisal. *It is strongly recommended that clients contact their insurance agent or under-writer regarding sales tax as a part of the cost of replacement, in order to determine whether or not it is covered in the insurance policy.*

**Role of the Appraiser** *("Appraiser" includes both Ralph Joseph Jewelers, and the undersigned)*

This appraisal report is not an offer to buy or sell the appraised item(s) at any price, nor is it a guarantee that the items are replaceable identically in the event of their loss. The stated value is not necessarily the same as the price at which the item would sell in this establishment.

Unless otherwise stated, the appraiser has no past, present or contemplated future interest in the appraised item(s), nor any other personal interest which would bias the report. Assignment of this appraisal and compensation for its performance are not contingent upon the values stated or the client's success or failure in the use of the report, nor is the estimated value based upon a percentage of stated value.

Unless otherwise stated, the property itemized in this appraisal was personally examined by the undersigned. If this appraisal report was prepared under environmental conditions which limit proper examination and evaluation of the item(s), the effects of such limitations on performance of the report will be explained.

**Documentation**

Photographs included in this report are for the purpose of design representation and documentation, and should not be relied upon for accurate color reproduction. Verbal color descriptions of colored stones, and diamond description and grading systems and nomenclature employed are those developed and promulgated by the Gemological Institute of America (GIA). At the appraiser's discretion, "Gemdialogue"™ or other color description system notations may also be used, in order to assist with color matching in the event of a loss.

A copy of the entire appraisal report, including notes and worksheets from which it was derived, will be retained in our files and held in the strictest confidence. It will not be released without the client's written consent unless we are legally compelled to provide access.

**Identification and Quantification of Materials**

Metal quality (i.e., 14K gold) is assumed to be consistent throughout a particular item, with that of the specific area tested and/or of the quality stamped or otherwise marked on the item, unless stated otherwise in the report. When testing is deemed necessary, it is either by the acid/scratch method, with an electronic testing device, or both. Either is generally accurate within 1 - 1.5 karat.

Unless otherwise stated, weights and measurements are estimates, based upon formulas and the use of measuring instruments as generally practiced and accepted in gemology and the jewelry appraisal profession.

Diamond grading is a subjective scientific procedure. Grades on the same diamond (particularly when mounted, and especially in yellow gold) may vary *slightly* from one professional, trained grader/appraiser to another, depending upon conditions of lighting, time allowed for grading, quality and accuracy of master (comparison) diamonds or non-diamond comparators if used, and color and hue discrimination abilities of the appraiser. Unless otherwise noted, the appraiser color graded any diamond(s) described in this appraisal using a GIA graded and registered diamond color comparison set containing diamonds graded E, G, I, K, M, and V-W, compared to the subject diamond(s) under a daylight equivalent diamond grading light.

Due to the limitations created by the mounting, *diamond color and clarity grades are provisional*, and might be changed by the undersigned if graded out of the mounting at a later date. Because of these limitations, diamonds which are mounted generally will not be assigned a "flawless" clarity grade (even provisionally), "ideal" cut assessment, or "D" color (highest color grade on the GIA grading scale). If a diamond is accompanied by a laboratory report prepared by the GIA Gem Trade Laboratory and can be verified as matching the report, the undersigned may defer to the GIA assessment.

## Condition

"*New*" denotes an item which is either brand new or shows a minute amount or no sign of wear or deterioration.  All gemstones are secure unless otherwise noted.

"*Normal wear*" denotes an item which contains scuffing, scratches, or other wear which would occur in the regular use of an item of the approximate age of the subject piece.  This designation generally indicates that the item might appear "like new" with light polishing and cleaning.

Other characteristics of condition may be described independently of the *normal wear* designation.

## Appraiser's Standards of Performance

This appraisal has been prepared in accordance with the report writing standards prescribed by the Best Society of Appraisers.  A statement of the appraiser's qualifications appears on Page 9 of this appraisal.

**Ralph Joseph Jewelers**

Respectfully submitted,

Ralph S. Joseph, ISA-CAPP
Graduate Gemologist (GIA)
President

# Ralph Joseph Jewelers

**91263 Diamond Blvd., Suite 5153**
**Hometown, New Jersey 08888**
**(609) 123-4567**

Appraisal prepared for:                                                          May 1, 1996

**Dr. and Mrs. Ross Stevens**
**918 Princeton Avenue**
**Harvard, New Jersey 08887**

## ITEM 1: DIAMOND ENGAGEMENT RING

LADIES' CONTEMPORARY 14 KARAT GOLD, DIAMOND SOLITAIRE ENGAGEMENT RING WITH A YELLOW GOLD SHANK AND A SIX PRONG WHITE GOLD HEAD, WITH POLISHED FINISH, OF TWO PIECE CAST CONSTRUCTION, THE ONE DIAMOND WEIGHING APPROXIMATELY 1.00 CARAT; THE SHANK IS STAMPED "c√j14K" AND "1.0 ct." (Check Mate Jewelry Mfg. Co., Providence, RI). THE TOTAL WEIGHT OF THE RING IS 2.13 DWT. (3.31 GRAMS).

Condition: Normal wear.

### The Diamond

| | |
|---|---|
| Diamond examined: | Mounted |
| Shape and cut: | Round, full cut modern brilliant |
| Approximate diameter: | 6.18 - 6.24 mm |
| Estimated depth: | 3.99 mm |
| ESTIMATED WEIGHT: | 1.00 CARAT (Manufacturer's stated weight, verified approximately by formulaic estimate) |
| COLOR: | J-K * |
| CLARITY: | $I_1$ |
| Estimated depth percentage: | 64.2% |
| Estimated table percentage: | 64.4% |
| Girdle thickness: | Extremely thick, faceted |
| Culet size: | Small |
| Estimated crown angle: | 35 degrees |
| Estimated pavilion depth: | 46% |
| Polish: | Good |
| Symmetry: | Good |
| Fluorescence: | None |
| Cut: | GIA Class 3 ("commercial") |

* Stated replacement value is based upon "J" color.

**ITEM 1, CONTINUED**

Plot Diagram of Diamond

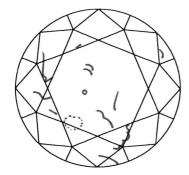 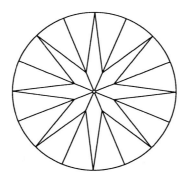

**Estimated retail replacement value:**          **$3,000.00**

**ITEM 2:  DIAMOND WEDDING BAND**

LADIES' CONTEMPORARY 14 KARAT YELLOW GOLD, "PYRAMID" ANNIVERSARY BAND, EACH DIAMOND SET WITH TWO PRONGS AT THE TIPS, WITH POLISHED FINISH, OF CAST CONSTRUCTION, THE RING CONTAINING SEVEN (7) DIAMONDS WEIGHING APPROXIMATELY 1.00 CARAT TOTAL (MANUFACTURER'S STATED WEIGHT); THE SHANK IS STAMPED "c√j14K" (Check Mate Jewelry Mfg. Co., Providence, RI).  THE TOTAL WEIGHT OF THE RING IS 1.84 DWT. (2.86 GRAMS).

Condition:  New.

The diamonds are marquise brilliants measuring approximately 5.0 x 2.5 mm through 5.5 x 2.8 mm.  They are approximately J through K color and $I_1$ clarity, with good polish and symmetry.

**Estimated retail replacement value:**          **$1,000.00**

## ITEM 3: ANTIQUE AMETHYST AND DIAMOND RING

LADIES' ANTIQUE (VICTORIAN, CIRCA 1890) 18 KARAT YELLOW GOLD RING WITH DIAMONDS BEAD AND PRONG SET IN STERLING SILVER, SURROUNDING ONE (1) NATURAL AMETHYST, THE RING TOP SUPPORTED BY A WIRE SCROLLWORK UNDERCARRIAGE, HAND FABRICATED, CONTAINING TWENTY-SIX (26) DIAMONDS WEIGHING APPROXIMATELY 0.35 CARAT TOTAL; THE SHANK IS NOT QUALITY STAMPED AND NO MAKER'S MARK IS APPARENT. THE TOTAL WEIGHT OF THE RING IS 2.81 DWT. (4.37 GRAMS).

Condition: Very good, less than normal wear, and gems are secure.

The diamonds are round, single cut, measuring approximately 1.0 through 1.7 mm in diameter. They are approximately I through K color and SI clarity, with fair to good polish and symmetry. The amethyst is a native cut, oval modified brilliant, measuring approximately 12.0 x 9.15 x 5.75 mm. It is transparent, medium light to light, moderately saturated purple, and lightly included, with good polish and symmetry. A window of approximately 30% is easily visible, as is prominent color zoning.

**Estimated retail replacement value:** **$850.00**

## VALUE SUMMARY

| | |
|---|---|
| **Total Estimated Retail Replacement Value, Three Items:** | **$4,850.00** |
| **6% New Jersey sales tax:** | **291.00** |
| **TOTAL:** | **$5,141.00** |

Ralph S. Joseph, ISA-CAPP
Graduate Gemologist (GIA)

Photographs, Items 1 and 2

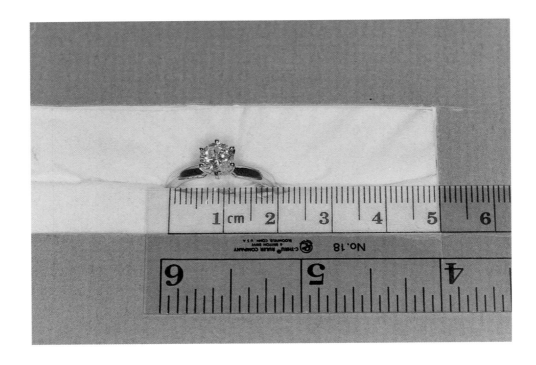

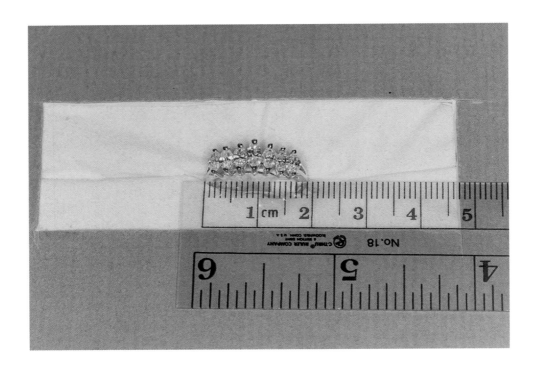

Photographs, Item 3

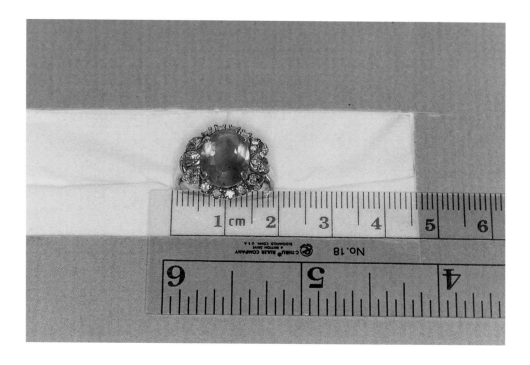

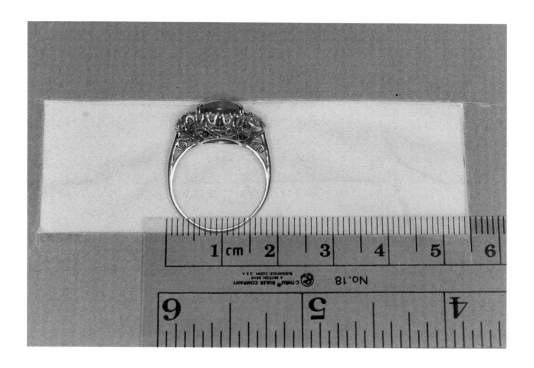

# RALPH S. JOSEPH - PROFESSIONAL PROFILE

## PROFESSIONAL EDUCATION AND DESIGNATIONS

GRADUATE GEMOLOGIST (GG) ★- Gemological Institute of America (Graduated 10/88)

CERTIFIED APPRAISER OF PERSONAL PROPERTY (CAPP) ★

Tested specialty in Antique and Period Jewelry - International Society of Appraisers and Indiana University (Certified 11/90)

Color Vision & Hue Discrimination tested, University of Chicago Visual Sciences Center
Color vision, normal          Hue discrimination, superior  (1995)
(Previously tested "normal to better" 1989)

Includes completion of, and exams passed for:
ISA 101: Professional Appraisal Practice
ISA 102: Appraiser's Fiduciary Responsibilities
ISA 103: Personal Property Methodology and Reasoning
ISA 10:   The Appraisal of Antique and Period Jewelry

CAPP Certification also includes passing a comprehensive final examination.

OTHER PROFESSIONAL EDUCATION COMPLETED
ISA 104: Advanced Appraisal Theory & Report Writing (5/90)
ISA 105: The Appraiser as Expert Witness and Pretrial Consultant (10/91)
Seminar: Understanding the Uniform Standards of Professional Appraisal Practice (USPAP)
... a Personal Property Perspective (National Appraisal Consultants - 4/95)

## AFFILIATIONS AND MEMBERSHIPS

BOARD OF DIRECTORS: Gem and Mineral Council, Los Angeles County
Museum of Natural History  (3/92 - 4/93)
EXECUTIVE BOARD: International Society of Appraisers, So. California Chapter (7/89 - 11/92)
GIA ALUMNI ASSOCIATION: Diploma Member
"THE JEWELRY SHOW": Creator and Co-host of live call-in talk show on KIEV-AM radio,
Los Angeles, CA (2/92 - 8/92)

## INDUSTRY BACKGROUND AND ACCOMPLISHMENTS

TWENTY-TWO YEARS IN THE JEWELRY INDUSTRY

AUTHOR: *The Jeweler's Guide to Effective Insurance Appraising*

APPRAISAL EDITOR and MONTHLY COLUMNIST: *National Jeweler* magazine (7/93 - present)

MEDIA AWARD Recipient, International Society of Appraisers for *National Jeweler* Column (3/95)

COURSE REVIEWER, for International Society of Appraisers (10/94)

INSTRUCTOR: International Society of Appraisers, in the CAPP Core Courses (7/92 - 10/93)

APPRAISER AND INSURANCE REPLACEMENT SPECIALIST: Employed in the retail jewelry
trade (2/93 - present)

PRESIDENT, RALPH JOSEPH GEMOLOGICAL SERVICES: Engaged in appraisals, consulting,
sales, and brokerage of gems and jewelry (1/90 - 1/93)

CEO, REGENCY JEWELRY CO., INC: Los Angeles, California (1984 - 1989), after employment
by same from 1972 - 1983

★ Indicates a title earned through formal education and testing.

**Ralph Joseph Jewelers**

# ADDENDUM
## DIAMOND GRADES EXPLAINED (GIA NOMENCLATURE)
("10X" Refers to Degree of Magnification)

## DIAMOND CLARITY

Fl—FLAWLESS: When examined by a trained grader under 10X, will show no blemishes or inclusions. The following would not disqualify a diamond from this category: 1. Extra facet on the pavilion, not visible when the diamond is face-up. 2. Naturals (unpolished part of the original crystal surface) which are confined to the girdle and do not thicken the girdle or distort its outline. 3. Internal graining (internal indications of irregular crystal growth, which may appear like faint streaks), which is not reflective, white, or colored and does not significantly affect transparency.

IF—INTERNALLY FLAWLESS: Shows no inclusions and only insignificant blemishes when examined under 10X. Blemishes generally are those which can be removed by minor repolishing.

VVS1 AND VVS2—VERY VERY SLIGHTLY INCLUDED: Contain minute inclusions that are difficult to locate under 10X, even for a skilled grader. In VVS1 they are extremely difficult to see, visible only from the pavilion, or possibly small and/or shallow enough to be polished out.

VS1 AND VS2—VERY SLIGHTLY INCLUDED: Contain minor inclusions which may be difficult (in VS1) to fairly easy (in VS2) to see, by a trained grader under 10X. Typical inclusions in VS diamonds are small feathers, small included crystals, and distinct clouds.

SI1 AND SI2—SLIGHTLY INCLUDED: Contain inclusions which are noticeable and easy (SI1) or very easy (SI2) to see under 10X. In some SI2 diamonds, inclusions are visible to the unaided eye if the stone is placed table down on a plain white background.

I1, I2, AND I3—"IMPERFECT": "I" grade diamonds contain inclusions which are very obvious to a trained grader under 10X and can usually be seen face up without magnification. In I1, beauty or durability are somewhat affected. In I2, beauty or durability are seriously affected. In I3, beauty and durability are seriously affected.

## DIAMOND COLOR

D - E - F: Colorless
G - H - I: Will "face up" colorless - even slight traces of color will not be apparent in mounted stones except to the trained eye.
J - K - L: Small diamonds will appear colorless "face up" when mounted, but larger ones will be tinted.
M - Z: Mounted diamonds display obvious tint, even to the untrained eye.

# ADDENDUM
## DIAMOND GRADES EXPLAINED (GIA NOMENCLATURE)
("10X" Refers to Degree of Magnification)

**ct.:** carat(s), a unit of gemstone weight. One carat = 0.2 gram. 7.777 carats = 1 pennyweight

**dwt.:** pennyweight, a unit of weight measurement. 20 dwt. = 1 troy ounce, and 12 troy ounces = 1 pound

**fluorescence:** the property of changing one kind of radiation to another, i.e., visible wavelengths exhibited by a material when it is excited by invisible radiation. When a diamond is fluorescent, it is most often blue, in reaction to long wave ultraviolet light.

**gram:** a unit of weight measurement. 1.5552 grams = 1 pennyweight

**inclusion:** (i.e., "lightly included"): any evidence of interruption of crystal growth - may be foreign solid matter, a "guest mineral" presence, or other internal characteristics including cracks, fractures, knots, clouds, bubbles, etc.

**k or karat:** denotes parts gold per 24 parts of metal: "14K" = 14/24, "18K" = 18/24, etc.

**modern brilliant cut diamond:** a style of cutting in which the octagonal table is surrounded by 32 facets above the girdle - it also contains 24 facets below the girdle (the culet is also considered to be a facet if the point is flattened).

**saturation:** the amount of hue present in a given color sensation - saturation is determined on a scale that runs from neutral to vivid.

**single cut diamond:** a modification of the brilliant, contain 17 or 18 facets - top of the stone consists of an octagonal table, surrounded by eight isosceles-trapezoid facets.

**sterling silver:** an alloy of 925/1000 silver.

**tone:** the sensation of the depth of color or darkness that is the result of blackness, saturation, or both - envision how a colored item would appear on black and white television - tone is divided into eleven steps of grey, from colorless or black.

**white gold:** karat gold alloyed with nickel, copper, and zinc - generally tougher and harder than yellow gold.

**yellow gold:** karat gold generally alloyed with copper and silver.

# Ralph Joseph Jewelers
## Consumer Survey - Appraisal Services

Dear valued client,

At Ralph Joseph Jewelers we endeavor to provide you with the best products, services, and value. Toward that end, we are very interested in your response to the appraisal services we performed for you recently. We would appreciate your taking the time to respond to this short questionnaire, and mail it to us in the attached self addressed, stamped envelope. We thank you in advance for providing this valuable feedback to us.

Sincerely,

Ralph S. Joseph
President

*Please circle the number that best represents the quality of service, five being best.*

1. Did our appraiser conduct a pre-appraisal interview in order to determine your needs?
   1  2  3  4  5
   Comments _____

2. Was your jewelry cleaned to your satisfaction?
   1  2  3  4  5
   Comments _____

3. Were your questions about the appraisal process answered to your satisfaction?
   1  2  3  4  5
   Comments _____

4. Was the gemological examination completed in a satisfactory time frame?
   1  2  3  4  5
   Comments _____

5. Was the finished appraisal delivered to you in a timely fashion?
   1  2  3  4  5
   Comments _____

6. Did you find the fee commensurate with the thoroughness and quality of the appraisal and consultation with our appraiser?
   1  2  3  4  5
   Comments _____

Do you have any other suggestions for improving this important service?

_____

_____

General comments: _____

actual cash value (ACV) policy  97

advocate, appraiser as  141

agreed value policy  23, 97

Altobelli, Cos  120

American Gem Society  110, 120

"Appraisal Days"  142

Appraisal Information Document  5, 23, 28, 48-55, 70-72

artist jewelry  36

assigned use  50

basis of value  50

Bevill, Bill  110

binding  77

brochures  110, 116

charitable contribution  132

civic groups  117

collateral  135

color vision  8

components  122

computers  74-76

"concealment or fraud" clause  99

condition  57

conflict of interest  139

conservatorship  134

consumer resale  133

contract for services  54, 65, 80

Coote, James  42

cost vs. value  39

cover letter  48

credentials  8

critical assumption  143

deposition  5

description, color systems  67

descriptions, colored stones  65, 66

descriptions, diamonds  61-65, 146

designer jewelry  36

diamond grading  55, 56

diamond grading nomenclature  60

diamond grading report, GIA/GTL  27

diamond grading reports  56

diamonds, Old Mine Cut  122-124

disclaimers  140, 146

disparagement  138

divorce  134

duplication  51, 120

enhancement disclosure  29

equitable distribution  134

fair market value  135

famous makers  121

fees  2, 110, 113, 140, 143, 147, 148

fees, contingency  4, 5, 140

fees, hourly  2

fees, minimum  4, 6

files  110, 111

fracture filled diamonds  29-31

Gemmological Association of Great Britain  16

Gemological Institute of America  26, 144, 147

gemology in appraising  60, 114

gemstone weights  55

GIA Gem Trade Laboratory  4, 56

glossary, use of  60

Guide, The  34

homeowner's insurance  112

hue  65

hypothetical appraisals  143

identification  54

independent appraisers  118

insurance advice  141

insurance replacement forms  104

insurance replacement forms, samples  105-107

insurance replacement procedures  102, 103

intended use  50

intensity  65

Internal Revenue Service  132

International Society of Appraisers  144

invoice, sample  3

laboratory reports  56

"like kind and quality"  13, 97

loss settlement  96

marketing, general  116, 117

marketing, to insurance companies  116, 117

markets, retail  42-45

markup  35

material facts  12, 18

metal fineness  54

Moody, Kevin  144

National Jeweler magazine  98, 110

one-of-a-kind items  120, 121

opals  122, 123

oral appraisals  142

pagination  48, 49

phone, selling on the  8

photographs, mounting  76-77

photography  8, 53, 67-69, 113

plotting diamonds  62-65

point of sale documentation  9, 12-18

Polygon  20

possible purchase, appraisal for  133

# Index

price guides  34
price lists  34
purpose and function  49
qualifications  114, 115, 144
qualifications, questions regarding  115
quantification  54
records  110, 111
reproduction cost/cost to reproduce  38
sales tax  51, 52
saturation  65
scheduled coverage  97
selling appraisals  111
societies, appraisal  148, 149
software, appraisal  74-76
Statement of Sale and Evaluation for Insurance  12
Statement of Sale and Evaluation
          for Insurance, sample  15, 16
Stone v. Those certain underwriters at Lloyds  17
take-in form  80-83
take-in form, sample  81, 82
tone  65
training, staff  7
updates  114
value vs. cost  39
values, overstated  22
verbal appraisals  114
watches  124, 125
worksheets  84, 85
worksheets, samples  86-93